SRA Reading Mastery

Signature Edition

Spelling Presentation Book
Grade K

Siegfried Engelmann
Elaine C. Bruner

McGraw Hill SRA

Columbus, OH

SRAonline.com

 SRA

Copyright © 2008 by SRA/McGraw-Hill.

All rights reserved. No part of this publication may be
reproduced or distributed in any form or by any means,
or stored in a database or retrieval system, without the
prior written consent of The McGraw-Hill Companies,
Inc., including, but not limited to, network storage or
transmission, or broadcast for distance learning.

Printed in the United States of America.

Send all inquiries to this address:
SRA/McGraw-Hill
4400 Easton Commons
Columbus, OH 43219

ISBN: 978-0-07-612231-8
MHID: 0-07-612231-X

5 6 7 8 9 RMN 13 12 11 10 09

The McGraw·Hill Companies

Guide to *Spelling Presentation Book* Grade K

Note: Do not begin the spelling activities with the first reading lesson.

Introduction

There are 111 lessons in the Spelling Presentation Book. Each lesson takes approximately 10 minutes to teach. If you are teaching small groups, present the first spelling lesson after a group completes **Lesson 50** in Presentation Book A. If you are teaching the entire class, you may start after the *lowest performing group* reaches **Lesson 40** in Presentation Book A. Do not include the spelling lesson as part of the reading period.

The children need the following skills to begin the spelling lessons:
1. identifying and writing the various sounds such as **m, t, s;**
2. "saying the sounds" in a word;
3. "saying a word fast."

Overview of Skills Taught

The spelling program is designed so that the children spell by sounds rather than by letter names. That is, they say the sounds in a word, then write the word.

In the early spelling lessons, the children write single sounds from dictation.

In Spelling Lesson 3, the children begin a more complex sound-writing exercise. The teacher dictates two sounds, with a pause between them. The children indicate what sound they are going to write first and what sound they are going to write next. Then the children write the sounds.

(Teachers are sometimes concerned that the children will begin pausing between sounds in their reading if pausing is introduced in the spelling. This response does not usually occur. The work with spelling facilitates the children's performance in reading.)

Beginning with Spelling Lesson 5, the children review saying the sounds in regularly spelled words. These words are presented orally.

Beginning with Spelling Lesson 9, the children combine the skills taught in previous lessons. They say the sounds in a word without pausing between the sounds. The teacher demonstrates how to say the sounds the "hard way," which involves saying the sounds with pauses between them. Finally, the children write the word.

At Spelling Lesson 33, the children start spelling words that are slightly irregular, such as **is** and **has.**

At Spelling Lesson 79, the children begin spelling irregular words such as **was** and **arm.**

Then, at Spelling Lesson 82, the children start writing an entire sentence from dictation. The children are responsible for remembering how to spell each of the words the right way.

General Procedures

Give each child lined paper and a pencil. Since each lesson takes only a few lines, you may want to collect the papers and pass them out daily until the page is filled.

It is preferable for children to write the dictated sounds in a row (across) instead of a column (down the paper).

Beginning at Spelling Lesson 9 and continuing through Spelling Lesson 111, a series of words is dictated. The children should write these words in a column (one word below the next).

Examples: Lessons 12, 61, and 83

12	61	83
n r n a t a n	ē	c
at	ron	was
it	and	tin
in	hit	did
	tan	we
	sit	we had sand.
	his	

Depending on the performance of the group you may be able to teach more than one spelling lesson per day and/or skip every fourth lesson. The criterion for accelerating or skipping is that the children make *very few* errors.

SPELLING LESSON 1

Note: Do not begin the spelling activities until the children have completed Lesson 50 in Presentation Book A. (See page 1.)

★ SOUND WRITING

Children write i and r

a. You're going to write some sounds.
b. Here's the first sound you're going to write.
   Listen. **iii.** What sound? (Signal.) *iii.*
c. Write **iii.** (Check children write **i.**)
d. Next sound. Listen. **rrr.** What sound? (Signal.) *rrr.*
e. Write **rrr.** (Check children write **r.**)
f. Next sound. Listen. **rrr.** What sound? (Signal.) *rrr.*
g. Write **rrr.** ✔
h. (Repeat steps *f* and *g* for the following sounds: **iii, rrr, iii.**)

SPELLING LESSON 2

SOUND WRITING

Children write r and i

a. You're going to write some sounds.
b. Here's the first sound you're going to write.
   Listen. **rrr.** What sound? (Signal.) *rrr.*
c. Write **rrr.** ✔
d. Next sound. Listen. **iii.** What sound? (Signal.) *iii.*
e. Write **iii.** ✔
f. Next sound. Listen. **iii.** What sound? (Signal.) *iii.*
g. Write **iii.** ✔
h. (Repeat steps *f* and *g* for the following sounds: **rrr, rrr, iii.**)

SPELLING LESSON 3

SOUND WRITING
EXERCISE 1

Children write r, a, and i

a. You're going to write some sounds.

b. Here's the first sound you're going to write.
   Listen. **rrr.** What sound? (Signal.) *rrr.*
c. Write **rrr.** ✔
d. Next sound. Listen. **aaa.** What sound? (Signal.) *aaa.*
e. Write **aaa.** ✔
f. Next sound. Listen. **iii.** What sound? (Signal.) *iii.*
g. Write **iii.** ✔
h. (Repeat steps *f* and *g* for the sound **aaa.**)

EXERCISE 2

Children write r a

a. Here are the sounds you're going to write next.
   Listen. **rrr** (pause two seconds) **aaa.**
b. Listen again. **rrr** (pause two seconds) **aaa.**
c. Your turn to say the sounds. Get ready. (Tap.) *rrr.* (Pause two seconds. Tap.) *aaa.*
• (Repeat until firm.)
d. What sound are you going to write first? (Signal.) *rrr.*
e. What sound are you going to write next? (Signal.) *aaa.*
f. (Repeat steps *d* and *e* until firm.)
g. Write **rrr** and **aaa.** ✔

SPELLING LESSON 4

SOUND WRITING
EXERCISE 1

Children write i, a, and r

a. You're going to write some sounds.
b. Here's the first sound you're going to write.
   Listen. **iii.** What sound? (Signal.) *iii.*
c. Write **iii.** ✔
d. Next sound. Listen. **aaa.** What sound? (Signal.) *aaa.*
e. Write **aaa.** ✔
f. Next sound. Listen. **rrr.** What sound? (Signal.) *rrr.*
g. Write **rrr.** ✔
h. (Repeat steps *f* and *g* for the sound **aaa.**)

EXERCISE 2

Children write r a

a. Here are the sounds you're going to write next.
   Listen. **rrr** (pause two seconds) **aaa.**
b. Listen again. **rrr** (pause two seconds) **aaa.**
c. Your turn to say the sounds. Get ready. (Tap.) *rrr.* (Pause two seconds. Tap.) *aaa.*
• (Repeat until firm.)
d. What sound are you going to write first? (Signal.) *rrr.*
e. What sound are you going to write next? (Signal.) *aaa.*
f. (Repeat steps *d* and *e* until firm.)
g. Write **rrr** and **aaa.** ✔

SPELLING LESSON 5

SOUND WRITING
EXERCISE 1

Children write r, i, and a

a. You're going to write some sounds.
b. Here's the first sound you're going to write. Listen. **rrr.** What sound? (Signal.) *rrr.*
c. Write **rrr.** ✔
d. Next sound. Listen. **iii.** What sound? (Signal.) *iii.*
e. Write **iii.** ✔
f. (Repeat steps *d* and *e* for the sounds **aaa** and **rrr.**)

EXERCISE 2

Children write a i

a. Here are the sounds you're going to write next. Listen. **aaa** (pause two seconds) **iii.**
b. Listen again. **aaa** (pause two seconds) **iii.**
c. Your turn to say the sounds. Get ready. (Tap.) *aaa.* (Pause two seconds. Tap.) *iii.*
• (Repeat until firm.)
d. What sound are you going to write first? (Signal.) *aaa.*
e. What sound are you going to write next? (Signal.) *iii.*
f. (Repeat steps *d* and *e* until firm.)
g. Write **aaa** and **iii.** ✔

★ SAY THE SOUNDS
EXERCISE 3

Children say the sounds in it, in

a. Listen. You're going to say the sounds in the word (pause) **it.**
b. What word? (Signal.) *It.* Yes, **it.**
c. (Hold up your hand.) Saying the sounds in (pause) **it.** Get ready. (Signal for **iii** and **t.**) (The children say *iiit* without pausing between the sounds.)
d. Again. (Repeat step *c* until firm.)
e. (When **iiit** is firm, say:) Say it fast. (Signal.) *It.*
f. Yes, what word? (Signal.) *It.*
• Good. You said the sounds in (pause) **it.**
g. (Repeat steps *a–f* for **in.**)

SPELLING LESSON 6

SOUND WRITING
EXERCISE 1

Children write a, i, and r

a. You're going to write some sounds.
b. Here's the first sound you're going to write. Listen. **aaa.** What sound? (Signal.) *aaa.*
c. Write **aaa.** ✔
d. Next sound. Listen. **iii.** What sound? (Signal.) *iii.*
e. Write **iii.** ✔
f. (Repeat steps *d* and *e* for the sounds **rrr** and **iii.**)

EXERCISE 2

Children write a r

a. Here are the sounds you're going to write next.
   Listen. **aaa** (pause two seconds) **rrr.**
b. Listen again. **aaa** (pause two seconds) **rrr.**
c. Your turn to say the sounds. Get ready. (Tap.) *aaa.* (Pause two seconds. Tap.) *rrr.*
• (Repeat until firm.)
d. What sound are you going to write first? (Signal.) *aaa.*
e. What sound are you going to write next? (Signal.) *rrr.*

f. (Repeat steps *d* and *e* until firm.)

g. Write **aaa** and **rrr.** ✔

★ SAY THE SOUNDS
EXERCISE 3

Children say the sounds in **at, in**

a. Listen. You're going to say the sounds in the word (pause) **at.**

b. What word? (Signal.) *At.* Yes, **at.**

c. (Hold up your hand.) Saying the sounds in (pause) **at.** Get ready. (Signal for **aaa** and **t.**) (The children say *aaat* without pausing between the sounds.)

d. Again. (Repeat until firm.)

e. (When **aaat** is firm, say:) Say it fast. (Signal.) *At.*

f. Yes, what word? (Signal.) *At.*

• Good. You said the sounds in (pause) **at.**

g. (Repeat steps *a–f* for **in.**)

SPELLING LESSON 7

SOUND WRITING
EXERCISE 1

Children write **t** and **r**

a. You're going to write some sounds.

b. Here's the first sound you're going to write.
Listen. **t.** What sound? (Signal.) *t.*

c. Write **t.** ✔

d. Next sound. Listen **rrr.** What sound? (Signal.) *rrr.*

e. Write **rrr.** ✔

EXERCISE 2

Children write **t a, t i**

a. Here are the sounds you're going to write next.
Listen. **t** (pause two seconds) **aaa.**

b. Listen again. **t** (pause two seconds) **aaa.**

c. Your turn to say the sounds. Get ready. (Tap.) *t.* (Pause two seconds. Tap.) *aaa.*

• (Repeat until firm.)

d. What sound are you going to write first? (Signal.) *t.*

e. What sound are you going to write next? (Signal.) *aaa.*

f. (Repeat steps *d* and *e* until firm.)

g. Write **t** and **aaa.** ✔

h. (Repeat steps *a–g* for the sounds **t iii.**)

SAY THE SOUNDS
EXERCISE 3

Children say the sounds in **it, an**

a. Listen. You're going to say the sounds in the word (pause) **it.**

b. What word? (Signal.) *It.* Yes, **it.**

c. (Hold up your hand.) Saying the sounds in (pause) **it.** Get ready. (Signal for **iii** and **t.**) (The children say *iiit* without pausing between the sounds.)

d. Again. (Repeat step *c* until firm.)

e. (When **iiit** is firm, say:) Say it fast. (Signal.) *It.*

f. Yes, what word? (Signal.) *It.*

• Good. You said the sounds in (pause) **it.**

g. (Repeat steps *a–f* for **an.**)

SPELLING LESSON 8

SOUND WRITING
EXERCISE 1

Children write **t** and **i**

a. You're going to write some sounds.

b. Here's the first sound you're going to write.
Listen. **t.** What sound? (Signal.) *t.*

c. Write **t.** ✔

d. Next sound. Listen. **iii.** What sound? (Signal.) *iii.*

e. Write **iii.** ✔

EXERCISE 2

Children write **t r, a t**

a. Here are the sounds you're going to write next.
Listen. **t** (pause two seconds) **rrr.**

b. Listen again. **t** (pause two seconds) **rrr.**

c. Your turn to say the sounds. Get ready. (Tap.) *t.* (Pause two seconds. Tap.) *rrr.*

• (Repeat step *c* until firm.)

d. What sound are you going to write first? (Signal.) *t.*

e. What sound are you going to write next? (Signal.) *rrr.*

f. (Repeat steps *d* and *e* until firm.)

g. Write **t** and **rrr.** ✔

h. (Repeat steps *a*–*g* for the sounds **aaa t.**)

SAY THE SOUNDS
EXERCISE 3

Children say the sounds in **am, it**

a. Listen. You're going to say the sounds in the word (pause) **am.**

b. What word? (Signal.) *Am.* Yes, **am.**

c. (Hold up your hand.) Saying the sounds in (pause) **am.** Get ready. (Signal for **aaa** and **m.**) (The children say *aaammm* without pausing between the sounds.)

d. Again. (Repeat step *c* until firm.)

e. (When **aaammm** is firm, say:) Say it fast. (Signal.) *Am.*

f. Yes, what word? (Signal.) *Am.*

• Good. You said the sounds in (pause) **am.**

g. (Repeat steps *a*–*f* for **it.**)

SPELLING LESSON 9

SOUND WRITING
EXERCISE 1

Children write **r i, t a, r t**

a. Here are the sounds you're going to write Listen. **rrr.** (pause two seconds) **iii.**

b. Listen again. **rrr** (pause two seconds) **iii.**

c. Your turn to say the sounds. Get ready. (Tap.) *rrr.* (Pause two seconds. Tap.) *iii.*

• (Repeat until firm.)

d. What sound are you going to write first? (Signal.) *rrr.*

e. What sound are you going to write next? (Signal.) *iii.*

f. (Repeat steps *d* and *e* until firm.)

g. Write **rrr** and **iii.** ✔

h. (Repeat steps *a*–*g* for the sounds **t aaa.**)

i. (Repeat steps *a*–*g* for the sounds **rrr t.**)

SAY THE SOUNDS
EXERCISE 2

Children say the sounds in **an, in**

a. Listen. You're going to say the sounds in the word (pause) **an.**

b. What word? (Signal.) *An.* Yes, **an.**

c. (Hold up your hand.) Saying the sounds in (pause) **an.** Get ready. (Signal for **aaa** and **nnn.**) (The children say *aaannn* without pausing between the sounds.)

d. Again. (Repeat step *c* until firm.)

e. (When **aaannn** is firm, say:) Say it fast. (Signal.) *An.*

f. Yes, what word? (Signal.) *An.*

• Good. You said the sounds in (pause) **an.**

g. (Repeat steps *a*–*f* for **in.**)

★ WORD WRITING
EXERCISE 3

Children write **it**

a. Everybody, get ready to say the sounds in (pause) **it.** Get ready. (Signal for each sound as the children say *iiit.*)

b. Let's do it the hard way. My turn. Saying the sounds in (pause) **it. iii** (pause two seconds) **t.** I said the sounds the hard way.

c. Do it with me. Saying the sounds in (pause) **it** the hard way. Get ready. (Signal for each sound as you and the children say:) *iii* (pause two seconds) *t.*

• (Repeat until firm.)

d. Your turn. All by yourselves. Saying the sounds in (pause) **it** the hard way. Get ready. (Signal for each sound as the children say:) *iii* (pause) *t.* (The children are to pause between the sounds.) Good.

e. Again. Saying the sounds in (pause) **it** the hard way. Get ready. (Signal for each sound as the children say:) *iii* (pause) *t.* (The children are to pause two seconds between the sounds.)

f. Everybody, write the sounds in (pause) **it.** ✔

• You wrote the word (pause) **it.** What word did you write? (Signal.) *It.*

Spelling Lesson 10

SOUND WRITING
EXERCISE 1

Children write n

a. You're going to write a sound.
b. Here's the sound you're going to write. Listen. **nnn.** What sound? (Signal.) *nnn.*
c. Write **nnn.** ✔

EXERCISE 2

Children write t r, n t

a. Here are the sounds you're going to write next. Listen. **t** (pause two seconds) **rrr.**
b. Listen again. **t** (pause two seconds) **rrr.**
c. Your turn to say the sounds. Get ready. (Tap.) *t.* (Pause two seconds. Tap.) *rrr.*
• (Repeat until firm.)
d. What sound are you going to write first? (Signal.) *t.*
e. What sound are you going to write next? (Signal.) *rrr.*
f. (Repeat steps *d* and *e* until firm.)
g. Write **t** and **rrr.** ✔
h. (Repeat steps *a–g* for the sounds **nnn t.**)

EXERCISE 3

Children write n a t

a. Here are some sounds you're going to write next. Listen. **nnn** (pause) **aaa** (pause) **t.**
b. Listen again. **nnn** (pause) **aaa** (pause) **t.**
c. Say the sounds with me. Get ready. (Tap for each sound as you and the children say:) *nnn* (pause) *aaa* (pause) *t.*
• (Repeat until firm.)
d. What sound are you going to write first? (Signal.) *nnn.*
e. What sound are you going to write next? (Signal.) *aaa.*
f. What sound are you going to write next? (Signal.) *t.*
g. (Repeat steps *d–f* until firm.)
h. Write **nnn** (pause) **aaa** (pause) **t.** ✔

SAY THE SOUNDS
EXERCISE 4

Children say the sounds in at, it

a. Listen. You're going to say the sounds in the word (pause) **at.**
b. What word? (Signal.) *At.* Yes, **at.**
c. (Hold up your hand.) Saying the sounds in (pause) **at.** Get ready. (Signal for **aaa** and **t.**) (The children say *aaat* without pausing between the sounds.)
d. Again. (Repeat until firm.)
e. (When **aaat** is firm, say:) Say it fast. (Signal.) *At.*
f. Yes, what word? (Signal.) *At.*
• Good. You said the sounds in (pause) **at.**
g. (Repeat steps *a–f* for **it.**)

WORD WRITING
EXERCISE 5

Children write it

a. Everybody, get ready to say the sounds in (pause) **it.** Get ready. (Signal for each sound as the children say *iiit.*)
b. Let's do it the hard way. My turn. Saying the sounds in (pause) **it. iii** (pause two seconds) **t.** I said the sounds the hard way.
c. Do it with me. Saying the sounds in (pause) **it** the hard way. Get ready. (Signal for each sound as you and the children say:) *iii* (pause two seconds) *t.*
• (Repeat until firm.)
d. Your turn. All by yourselves. Saying the sounds in (pause) **it** the hard way. (Signal for each sound as the children say:) *iii* (pause) *t.* (The children are to pause between the sounds.) Good.
e. Again. Saying the sounds in (pause) **it** the hard way. Get ready. (Signal for each sound as the children say:) *iii* (pause) *t.* (The children are to pause two seconds between the sounds.)
f. Everybody, write the sounds in (pause) **it.** ✔ You wrote the word (pause) **it.**
• What word did you write? (Signal.) *It.*

WORD WRITING
EXERCISE 6

Children write at

a. Everybody, get ready to say the sounds in (pause) **at.** Get ready. (Signal for each sound as the children say:) *aaat.*

b. Let's do it the hard way. My turn. Saying the sounds in (pause) **at. Aaa** (pause) **t.** I said the sounds the hard way.

c. Do it with me. Saying the sounds in (pause) **at** the hard way. Get ready. (Signal for each sound as you and the children say:) *aaa* (pause two seconds) *t.*
• (Repeat until firm.)

d. Your turn. All by yourselves. Saying the sounds in (pause) **at** the hard way. Get ready. (Signal for each sound as the children say:) *aaa* (pause) *t.* (The children are to pause between the sounds.) Good.

e. Again. Saying the sounds in (pause) **at** the hard way. Get ready. (Signal for each sound as the children say:) *aaa* (pause) *t.* (The children are to pause two seconds between the sounds.)

f. Everybody, write the sounds in (pause) **at.** ✔
• You wrote the word (pause) **at.** What word did you write? (Signal.) *At.*

SPELLING LESSON 11

SOUND WRITING
EXERCISE 1

Children write n i, r t

a. Here are the sounds you're going to write. Listen. **nnn** (pause two seconds) **iii.**

b. Listen again. **nnn** (pause two seconds) **iii.**

c. Your turn to say the sounds. Get ready. (Tap.) *nnn.* (Pause two seconds. Tap.) *iii.*
• (Repeat until firm.)

d. What sound are you going to write first? (Signal.) *nnn.*

e. What sound are you going to write next? (Signal.) *iii.*

f. (Repeat steps *d* and *e* until firm.)

g. Write **nnn** and **iii.** ✔

h. (Repeat steps *a–g* for **rrr t.**)

EXERCISE 2

Children write t a n

a. Here are some sounds you're going to write next.
Listen. **t** (pause) **aaa** (pause) **nnn.**

b. Listen again. **t** (pause) **aaa** (pause) **nnn.**

c. Say the sounds with me. Get ready. (Tap for each sound as you and the children say:) *t* (pause) *aaa* (pause) *nnn.*
• (Repeat until firm.)

d. What sound are you going to write first? (Signal.) *t.*

e. What sound are you going to write next? (Signal.) *aaa.*

f. What sound are you going to write next? (Signal.) *nnn.*

g. (Repeat steps *d–f* until firm.)

h. Write **t** (pause) **aaa** (pause) **nnn.** ✔

SAY THE SOUNDS
EXERCISE 3

Children say the sounds in in, an

a. Listen. You're going to say the sounds in the word (pause) **in.**

b. What word? (Signal.) *In.* Yes, **in.**

c. (Hold up your hand.) Saying the sounds in (pause) **in.** Get ready. (Signal for **i** and **n.**) (The children say *iiinnn* without pausing between the sounds.)

d. Again. (Repeat *c* until firm.)

e. (When **iiinnn** is firm, say:) Say it fast. (Signal.) *In.*

f. Yes, what word? (Signal.) *In.*
• Good. You said the sounds in (pause) **in.**

g. (Repeat steps *a–f* for **an.**)

WORD WRITING
EXERCISE 4

Children write at

a. Everybody, get ready to say the sounds in (pause) **at.** Get ready. (Signal for each sound as the children say:) *aaat.*

b. Let's do it the hard way. My turn. Saying the sounds in (pause) **at. Aaa** (pause) **t.** I said the sounds the hard way.

c. Do it with me. Saying the sounds in (pause) **at** the hard way. Get ready. (Signal for each sound as you and the children say:) *aaa* (pause two seconds) *t.*
• (Repeat until firm.)
d. Your turn. All by yourselves. Saying the sounds in (pause) **at** the hard way. Get ready. (Signal for each sound as the children say:) *aaa* (pause) *t.* (The children are to pause between the sounds.) Good.
e. Again. Saying the sounds in (pause) **at** the hard way. Get ready. (Signal for each sound as the children say:) *aaa* (pause) *t.* (The children are to pause between the sounds.)
f. Everybody, write the sounds in (pause) **at.** ✔
You wrote the word (pause) **at.**
• What word did you write? (Signal.) *At.*

EXERCISE 5

Children write it

a. Everybody, get ready to say the sounds in (pause) **it.** Get ready. (Signal for each sound as the children say:) *iiit.*
b. Let's do it the hard way. My turn. Saying the sounds in (pause) **it. iii** (pause) **t.**
I said the sounds the hard way.
c. Do it with me. Saying the sounds in (pause) **it** the hard way. Get ready. (Signal for each sound as you and the children say:) *iii* (pause two seconds) *t.*
• (Repeat until firm.)
d. Your turn. All by yourselves. Saying the sounds in (pause) **it** the hard way. Get ready. (Signal for each sound as the children say:) *iii* (pause) *t.* (The children are to pause between the sounds.) Good.
e. Again. Saying the sounds in (pause) **it** the hard way. Get ready. (Signal for each sound as the children say:) *iii* (pause) *t.* (The children are to pause between the sounds.)

f. Everybody, write the sounds in (pause) **it.** ✔
You wrote the word (pause) **it.** What did you write? (Signal.) *It.*

SPELLING LESSON 12

SOUND WRITING
EXERCISE 1

Children write n r, n a

a. Here are the sounds you're going to write. Listen. **nnn** (pause two seconds) **rrr.**
b. Listen again. **nnn** (pause two seconds) **rrr.**
c. Your turn to say the sounds. Get ready. (Tap.) *nnn.* (Pause two seconds. Tap.) *rrr.*
• (Repeat until firm.)
d. What sound are you going to write first? (Signal.) *nnn.*
e. What sound are you going to write next? (Signal.) *rrr.*
f. (Repeat steps *d* and *e* until firm.)
g. Write **nnn** and **rrr.** ✔
h. (Repeat steps *a–g* for **nnn aaa.**)

EXERCISE 2

Children write t a n

a. Here are some sounds you're going to write next. Listen. **t** (pause) **aaa** (pause) **nnn.**
b. Listen again. **t** (pause) **aaa** (pause) **nnn.**
c. Say the sounds with me. Get ready. (Tap for each sound as you and the children say:) *t* (pause) *aaa* (pause) *nnn.*
• (Repeat until firm.)
d. What sound are you going to write first? (Signal.) *t.*
e. What sound are you going to write next? (Signal.) *aaa.*
f. What sound are you going to write next? (Signal.) *nnn.*
g. (Repeat steps *d–f* until firm.)
h. Write **t** (pause) **aaa** (pause) **nnn.** ✔

WORD WRITING
EXERCISE 3

Children write at

a. You're going to write the word (pause) **at.** First you're going to say the sounds. Then you're going to write the word.

b. Saying the sounds in (pause) **at.** Get ready. (Signal for each sound as the children say:) *aaat.*

c. Now you're going to say the sounds the hard way. Saying the sounds in (pause) **at.** Get ready. (Signal for each sound as the children say:) *aaa* (pause) *t.* (The children are to pause two seconds between the sounds.)

d. (Repeat step *c* until firm.)

e. Everybody, write the word (pause) **at.** ✔

• What word did you write? (Signal.) *At.*

EXERCISE 4

Children write it

a. You're going to write the word (pause) **it.** First you're going to say the sounds. Then you're going to write the word.

b. Saying the sounds in (pause) **it.** Get ready. (Signal for each sound as the children say:) *iiit.*

c. Now you're going to say the sounds the hard way. Saying the sounds in (pause) **it.** Get ready. (Signal for each sound as the children say:) *iii* (pause) *t.* (The children are to pause two seconds between the sounds.)

d. (Repeat step *c* until firm.)

e. Everybody, write the word (pause) **it.** ✔

• What word did you write? (Signal.) *It.*

EXERCISE 5

Children write in

a. You're going to write the word (pause) **in.** First you're going to say the sounds. Then you're going to write the word.

b. Saying the sounds in (pause) **in.** Get ready. (Signal for each sound as the children say:) *iiinnn.*

c. Now you're going to say the sounds the hard way. Saying the sounds in (pause) **in.** Get ready. (Signal for each sound as the children say:) *iii* (pause) *nnn.* (The children are to pause two seconds between the sounds.)

d. (Repeat step *c* until firm.)

e. Everybody, write the word (pause) **in.** ✔

• What word did you write? (Signal.) *In.*

SPELLING LESSON 13

SOUND WRITING
EXERCISE 1

Children write f

a. You're going to write a sound.

b. Here's the sound you're going to write. Listen. **fff.** What sound? (Signal.) *fff.*

c. Write **fff.** ✔

EXERCISE 2

Children write r f t, f a i

a. Here are some sounds you're going to write next. Listen. **rrr** (pause) **fff** (pause) **t.**

b. Listen again. **rrr** (pause) **fff** (pause) **t.**

c. Say the sounds with me. Get ready. (Tap for each sound as you and the children say:) *rrr* (pause) *fff* (pause) *t.*

• (Repeat until firm.)

d. What sound are you going to write first? (Signal.) *rrr.*

e. What sound are you going to write next? (Signal.) *fff.*

f. What sound are you going to write next? (Signal.) *t.*

g. (Repeat steps *d–f* until firm.)

h. Write **rrr** (pause) **fff** (pause) **t.** ✔

i. (Repeat steps *a–h* for **fff aaa iii.**)

WORD WRITING
EXERCISE 3

Children write an, in, at

a. You're going to write the word (pause) **an.** First you're going to say the sounds. Then you're going to write the word.

b. Saying the sounds in (pause) **an.** Get ready. (Signal for each sound as the children say:) *aaannn.*

c. Now you're going to say the sounds the hard way. Saying the sounds in (pause) **an.** Get ready. (Signal for each sound as the children say:) *aaa* (pause) *nnn.* (The children are to pause two seconds between the sounds.)

d. (Repeat step *c* until firm.)

e. Everybody, write the word (pause) **an.** ✔

• What word did you write? (Signal.) *An.*

f. (Repeat steps *a–e* for **in** and **at.**)

SPELLING LESSON 14

SOUND WRITING
EXERCISE 1

Children write **f i n, f a n, f i t**

a. Here are some sounds you're going to write. Listen. **fff** (pause) **iii** (pause) **nnn.**

b. Listen again. **fff** (pause) **iii** (pause) **nnn.**

c. Say the sounds with me. Get ready. (Tap for each sound as you and the children say:) *fff* (pause) *iii* (pause) *nnn.*

• (Repeat until firm.)

d. What sound are you going to write first? (Signal.) *fff.*

e. What sound are you going to write next? (Signal.) *iii.*

f. What sound are you going to write next? (Signal.) *nnn.*

g. (Repeat steps *d–f* until firm.)

h. Write **fff** (pause) **iii** (pause) **nnn.** ✔

i. (Repeat steps *a–h* for **fff aaa nnn.**)

j. (Repeat steps *a–h* for **fff iii ttt.**)

WORD WRITING
EXERCISE 2

Children write **at, it, rat**

a. You're going to write the word (pause) **at.** First you're going to say the sounds. Then you're going to write the word.

b. Saying the sounds in (pause) **at.** Get ready. (Signal for each sound as the children say:) *aaat.*

c. Now you're going to say the sounds the hard way. Saying the sounds in (pause) **at.** Get ready. (Signal for each sound as the children say:) *aaa* (pause) *t.* (The children are to pause two seconds between the sounds.)

d. (Repeat *c* until firm.)

e. Everybody, write the word (pause) **at.** ✔

• What word did you write? (Signal.) *At.*

f. (Repeat steps *a–e* for **it** and **rat.**)

SPELLING LESSON 15

SOUND WRITING
EXERCISE 1

Children write **f a n, f a t**

a. Here are some sounds you're going to write. Listen. **fff** (pause) **aaa** (pause) **nnn.**

b. Listen again. **fff** (pause) **aaa** (pause) **nnn.**

c. Say the sounds with me. Get ready. (Tap for each sound as you and the children say:) *fff* (pause) *aaa* (pause) *nnn.*

• (Repeat until firm.)

d. What sound are you going to write first? (Signal.) *fff.*

e. What sound are you going to write next? (Signal.) *aaa.*

f. What sound are you going to write next? (Signal.) *nnn.*

g. (Repeat steps *d–f* until firm.)

h. Write **fff** (pause) **aaa** (pause) **nnn.** ✔

i. (Repeat steps *a–h* for **fff aaa ttt.**)

WORD WRITING
EXERCISE 2

Children write **if, in**

a. You're going to write the word (pause) **if.** First you're going to say the sounds. Then you're going to write the word.

b. Saying the sounds in (pause) **if.** Get ready. (Signal for each sound as the children say:) *iiifff.*

c. Now you're going to say the sounds the hard way. Saying the sounds in (pause) **if.** Get ready. (Signal for each sound as the children say:) *iii* (pause) *fff.* (The children are to pause two seconds between the sounds.)

d. (Repeat step *c* until firm.)

e. Everybody, write the word (pause) **if.** ✔

• What word did you write? (Signal.) *If.*

f. (Repeat steps *a–e* for **in.**)

EXERCISE 3

Children write **it, rat**

a. You're going to write the word **it.** Listen: **it.** Saying the sounds in (pause) **it** the hard way. Get ready. (Signal for each sound as the children say:) *iii* (pause) *t.*

• (The children are to pause two seconds between the sounds.)

• (Repeat until firm.)

b. Everybody, write the word (pause) **it.** ✔

c. Now you're going to write the word **rat.** Listen. **Rat.** Saying the sounds the hard way. Get ready. (Signal for each sound as the children say:) *rrr* (pause) *aaa* (pause) *t.* (The children are to pause two seconds between the sounds.)

• (Repeat until firm.)

d. Everybody, write the word (pause) **rat.** ✔

SPELLING LESSON 16

SOUND WRITING
EXERCISE 1

Children write **o**

a. You're going to write a sound.

b. Here's the sound you're going to write. Listen. **ooo.** What sound? (Signal.) *ooo.*

c. Write **ooo.** ✔

EXERCISE 2

Children write **t i o, n o f**

a. Here are some sounds you're going to write next. Listen. **t** (pause) **iii** (pause) **ooo.**

b. Listen again. **t** (pause) **iii** (pause) **ooo.**

c. Say the sounds with me. Get ready. (Tap for each sound as you and the children say:) *t* (pause) *iii* (pause) *ooo.*

• (Repeat until firm.)

d. What sound are you going to write first? (Signal.) *t.*

e. What sound are you going to write next? (Signal.) *iii.*

f. What sound are you going to write next? (Signal.) *ooo.*

g. (Repeat steps *d–f* until firm.)

h. Write **t** (pause) **iii** (pause) **ooo.** ✔

i. (Repeat steps *a–h* for **nnn ooo fff.**)

WORD WRITING
EXERCISE 3

Children write **an, fan, it**

a. You're going to write the word **an.** Saying the sounds the hard way. Get ready. (Signal for each sound as the children say:) *aaa* (pause) *nnn.* (The children are to pause two seconds between the sounds.)

• (Repeat until firm.)

b. Everybody, write the word (pause) **an.**

c. (Repeat steps *a* and *b* for **fan** and **it.**)

SPELLING LESSON 17

SOUND WRITING
EXERCISE 1

Children write **o t i, r o t**

a. Here are some sounds you're going to write. Listen. **ooo** (pause) **t** (pause) **iii.**

b. Listen again. **ooo** (pause) **t** (pause) **iii.**

c. Say the sounds with me. Get ready. (Tap for each sound as you and the children say:) *ooo* (pause) *t* (pause) *iii.*

• (Repeat until firm.)

d. What sound are you going to write first? (Signal.) *ooo.*

e. What sound are you going to write next? (Signal.) *t.*

f. What sound are you going to write next? (Signal.) *iii.*

g. (Repeat steps *d–f* until firm.)

h. Write **ooo** (pause) **t** (pause) **iii.** ✔

i. (Repeat steps *a–h* for **rrr ooo t.**)

WORD WRITING
EXERCISE 2

Children write an, fan, at, fat

a. You're going to write the word **an.** Listen. **An.** Saying the sounds the hard way. Get ready. (Signal for each sound as the children say:) *aaa* (pause) *nnn.* (The children are to pause two seconds between the sounds.)

• (Repeat until firm.)

b. Everybody, write the word (pause) **an.** ✔

c. (Repeat steps *a* and *b* for **fan, at,** and **fat.**)

SPELLING LESSON 18

SOUND WRITING
EXERCISE 1

Children write n o t, n a f

a. Here are some sounds you're going to write. Listen. **nnn** (pause) **ooo** (pause) **t.**

b. Listen again. **nnn** (pause) **ooo** (pause) **t.**

c. Say the sounds with me. Get ready. (Tap for each sound as you and the children say:) *nnn* (pause) *ooo* (pause) *t.*

• (Repeat until firm.)

d. What sound are you going to write first? (Signal.) *nnn.*

e. What sound are you going to write next? (Signal.) *ooo.*

f. What sound are you going to write next? (Signal.) *t.*

g. (Repeat steps *d–f* until firm.)

h. Write **nnn** (pause) **ooo** (pause) **t.** ✔

i. (Repeat steps *a–h* for **nnn aaa fff.**)

WORD WRITING
EXERCISE 2

Children write in, fin, an, fan

a. You're going to write the word **in.** Listen: **in.** Saying the sounds the hard way. Get ready. (Signal for each sound as the children say:) *iii* (pause) *nnn.* (The children are to pause two seconds between the sounds.)

• (Repeat until firm.)

b. Everybody, write the word (pause) **in.** ✔

c. (Repeat steps *a* and *b* for **fin, an,** and **fan.**)

SPELLING LESSON 19

SOUND WRITING
EXERCISE 1

Children write a n a, t o n

a. Here are some sounds you're going to write. Listen. **aaa** (pause) **nnn** (pause) **aaa.**

b. Listen again. **aaa** (pause) **nnn** (pause) **aaa.**

c. Say the sounds with me. Get ready. (Tap for each sound as you and the children say:) *aaa* (pause) *nnn* (pause) *aaa.*

• (Repeat until firm.)

d. What sound are you going to write first? (Signal.) *aaa.*

e. What sound are you going to write next? (Signal.) *nnn.*

f. What sound are you going to write next? (Signal.) *aaa.*

g. (Repeat steps *d–f* until firm.)

h. Write **aaa** (pause) **nnn** (pause) **aaa.** ✔

i. (Repeat steps *a–h* for **t ooo nnn.**)

WORD WRITING
EXERCISE 2

Children write rat, if, it, in

a. You're going to write the word **rat.** Listen. **Rat.** Saying the sounds the hard way. Get ready. (Signal for each sound as the children say:) *rrr* (pause) *aaa* (pause) *t.* (The children are to pause two seconds between the sounds.)

• (Repeat until firm.)

b. Everybody, write the word (pause) **rat.** ✔

c. (Repeat steps *a* and *b* for **if, it,** and **in.**)

SPELLING LESSON 20

SOUND WRITING
EXERCISE 1

Children write m

a. You're going to write a sound.

b. Here's the sound you're going to write. Listen. **mmm.** What sound? (Signal.) *mmm.*

c. Write **mmm.** ✔

EXERCISE 2

Children write a n m, o m i

a. Here are some sounds you're going to write next. Listen. **aaa** (pause) **nnn** (pause) **mmm.**

b. Listen again. **aaa** (pause) **nnn** (pause) **mmm.**

c. Say the sounds with me. Get ready. (Tap for each sound as you and the children say:) *aaa* (pause) *nnn* (pause) *mmm.*

• (Repeat until firm.)

d. What sound are you going to write first? (Signal.) *aaa.*

e. What sound are you going to write next? (Signal.) *nnn.*

f. What sound are you going to write next? (Signal.) *mmm.*

g. (Repeat steps *d–f* until firm.)

h. Write **aaa** (pause) **nnn** (pause) **mmm.** ✔

i. (Repeat steps *a–h* for **ooo mmm iii.**)

SOUND WRITING
EXERCISE 3

Children write an, fan, ran, if

a. You're going to write the word **an.** Listen. **An.** Saying the sounds the hard way. Get ready. (Signal for each sound as the children say:) *aaa* (pause) *nnn.* (The children are to pause two seconds between the sounds.)

• (Repeat until firm.)

b. Everybody, write the word (pause) **an.** ✔

c. (Repeat steps *a* and *b* for **fan, ran,** and **if.**)

SPELLING LESSON 21

SOUND WRITING
EXERCISE 1

Children write o m i, f m t

a. Here are some sounds you're going to write. Listen. **ooo** (pause) **mmm** (pause) **iii.**

b. Listen again. **ooo** (pause) **mmm** (pause) **iii.**

c. Say the sounds with me. Get ready. (Tap for each sound as you and the children say:) *ooo* (pause) *mmm* (pause) *iii.*

• (Repeat until firm.)

d. What sound are you going to write first? (Signal.) *ooo.*

e. What sound are you going to write next? (Signal.) *mmm.*

f. What sound are you going to write next? (Signal.) *iii.*

g. (Repeat steps *d–f* until firm.)

h. Write **ooo** (pause) **mmm** (pause) **iii.** ✔

i. (Repeat steps *a–h* for **fff mmm t.**)

WORD WRITING
EXERCISE 2

Children write it

You're going to write the word **it.** Think about the sounds in (pause) **it** and write the word. ✔

> **To Correct**
> 1. Say the sounds in **it.** (Signal.) *iiit.*
> 2. Say the sounds the hard way. (Signal.) *iii* (pause) *t.*
> 3. Write the word **it.** ✔

EXERCISE 3

Children write fit

a. Now you're going to write the word **fit.** Listen. **Fit.** Saying the sounds the hard way. Get ready. (Signal for each sound as the children say:) *fff* (pause) *iii* pause) *t.* (The children are to pause two seconds between the sounds.)

• (Repeat until firm.)

b. Everybody, write the word (pause) **fit.** ✔

EXERCISE 4

Children write at

You're going to write the word **at.** Think about the sounds in (pause) **at** and write the word. ✔

EXERCISE 5

Children write fat

a. Now you're going to write the word **fat.** Listen. **Fat.** Saying the sounds the hard way. Get ready. (Signal for each sound as the children say:) *fff* (pause) *aaa* (pause) *t.* (The children are to pause two seconds between the sounds.)

- (Repeat until firm.)
b. Everybody, write the word (pause) **fat.** ✔

SPELLING LESSON 22

SOUND WRITING
EXERCISE 1

Children write **o n m, a t m**

a. Here are some sounds you're going to write. Listen. **ooo** (pause) **nnn** (pause) **mmm.**

b. Listen again. **ooo** (pause) **nnn** (pause) **mmm.**

c. Say the sounds with me. Get ready. (Tap for each sound as you and the children say:) *ooo* (pause) *nnn* (pause) *mmm.*

- (Repeat until firm.)

d. What sound are you going to write first? (Signal.) *ooo.*

e. What sound are you going to write next? (Signal.) *nnn.*

f. What sound are you going to write next? (Signal.) *mmm.*

g. (Repeat steps *d–f* until firm.)

h. Write **ooo** (pause) **nnn** (pause) **mmm.** ✔

i. (Repeat steps *a–h* for **aaa t mmm.**)

WORD WRITING
EXERCISE 2

Children write **in**

You're going to write the word **in.** Think about the sounds in (pause) **in** and write the word. ✔

> **To Correct**
> 1. Say the sounds in **in.** (Signal.) *iiinnn.*
> 2. Say the sounds the hard way. (Signal.) *iii* (pause) *nnn.*
> 3. Write the word **in.** ✔

EXERCISE 3

Children write **fin**

a. Now you're going to write the word **fin.** Listen. **Fin.** Saying the sounds the hard way. Get ready. (Signal for each sound as the children say:) *fff* (pause) *iii* (pause) *nnn.* (The children are to pause two seconds between the sounds.)

- (Repeat until firm.)
b. Everybody, write the word (pause) **fin.** ✔

EXERCISE 4

Children write **an**

You're going to write the word **an.** Think about the sounds in (pause) **an** and write the word. ✔

EXERCISE 5

Children write **ran**

a. Now you're going to write the word **ran.** Listen. **Ran.** Saying the sounds the hard way. Get ready. (Signal for each sound as the children say:) *rrr* (pause) *aaa* (pause) *nnn.* (The children are to pause two seconds between the sounds.)

- (Repeat until firm.)
b. Everybody, write the word (pause) **ran.** ✔

SPELLING LESSON 23

SOUND WRITING
EXERCISE 1

Children write **m n o, n m r**

a. Here are some sounds you're going to write. Listen. **mmm** (pause) **nnn** (pause) **ooo.**

b. Listen again. **mmm** (pause) **nnn** (pause) **ooo.**

c. Say the sounds with me. Get ready. (Tap for each sound as you and the children say:) *mmm* (pause) *nnn* (pause) *ooo.*

- (Repeat until firm.)

d. What sound are you going to write first? (Signal.) *mmm.*

e. What sound are you going to write next? (Signal.) *nnn.*

f. What sound are you going to write next? (Signal.) *ooo.*

g. (Repeat steps *d–f* until firm.)

h. Write **mmm** (pause) **nnn** (pause) **ooo.** ✔

i. (Repeat steps *a–h* for **nnn mmm rrr.**)

WORD WRITING
EXERCISE 2

Children write **an**

You're going to write the word **an.** Think about the sounds in (pause) **an** and write the word. ✔

> ### To Correct
>
> 1. Say the sounds in **an.** (Signal.) *aaannn.*
> 2. Say the sounds the hard way. (Signal.) *aaa* (pause) *nnn.*
> 3. Write the word **an.** ✔

EXERCISE 3

Children write **fan, ran, man**

a. Now you're going to write the word **fan.** Listen. **Fan.** Saying the sounds the hard way. Get ready. (Signal for each sound as the children say:) *fff* (pause) *aaa* (pause) *nnn.* (The children are to pause two seconds between sounds.)
- (Repeat until firm.)
b. Everybody, write the word (pause) **fan.** ✔
c. (Repeat steps *a* and *b* for **ran** and **man**.)

SPELLING LESSON 24

SOUND WRITING
EXERCISE 1

Children write **o t m, f r i**

a. Here are some sounds you're going to write. Listen. **ooo** (pause) **t** (pause) **mmm.**
b. Listen again. **ooo.** (pause) **t** (pause) **mmm.**
c. Say the sounds with me. Get ready. (Tap for each sound as you and the children say:) *ooo* (pause) *t* (pause) *mmm.*
- (Repeat until firm.)
d. What sound are you going to write first? (Signal.) *ooo.*
e. What sound are you going to write next? (Signal.) *t.*
f. What sound are you going to write next? (Signal.) *mmm.*
g. (Repeat steps *d–f* until firm.)

h. Write **ooo** (pause) **t** (pause) **mmm.** ✔
i. (Repeat steps *a–h* for **fff rrr iii.**)

WORD WRITING
EXERCISE 2

Children write **at**

You're going to write the word **at.** Think about the sounds in (pause) **at** and write the word. ✔

> ### To Correct
>
> 1. Say the sounds in **at.** (Signal.) *aaat.*
> 2. Say the sounds the hard way. (Signal.) *aaa* (pause) *t.*
> 3. Write the word **at.** ✔

EXERCISE 3

Children write **mat**

a. You're going to write the word **mat.** Listen. **Mat.** Saying the sounds in (pause) **mat** the hard way. Get ready. (Signal for each sound as the children say:) *mmm* (pause) *aaa* (pause) *t.* (The children are to pause two seconds between the sounds.)
- (Repeat until firm.)
b. Everybody, write the word (pause) **mat.** ✔

EXERCISE 4

Children write **am**

You're going to write the word **am.** Think about the sounds in (pause) **am** and write the word. ✔

EXERCISE 5

Children write **ram**

a. You're going to write the word **ram.** Listen. **Ram.** Saying the sounds in (pause) **ram** the hard way. Get ready. (Signal for each sound as the children say:) *rrr* (pause) *aaa* (pause) *mmm.* (The children are to pause two seconds between the sounds.)
- (Repeat until firm.)
b. Everybody, write the word (pause) **ram.** ✔

EXERCISE 6

Children write in

You're going to write the word **in.** Think about the sounds in (pause) **in** and write the word. ✔

Spelling Lesson 25

SOUND WRITING
EXERCISE 1

Children write a m i

a. Here are some sounds you're going to write. Listen. **aaa** (pause) **mmm** (pause) **iii.**

b. Listen again. **aaa** (pause) **mmm** (pause) **iii.**

c. Say the sounds with me. Get ready. (Tap for each sound as you and the children say:) *aaa* (pause) *mmm* (pause) *iii.*

• (Repeat until firm.)

d. What sound are you going to write first? (Signal.) *aaa.*

e. What sound are you going to write next? (Signal.) *mmm.*

f. What sound are you going to write next? (Signal.) *iii.*

g. (Repeat steps *d–f* until firm.)

h. Write **aaa** (pause) **mmm** (pause) **iii.** ✔

WORD WRITING
EXERCISE 2

Children write if, it

a. You're going to write the word **if.** Think about the sounds in (pause) **if** and write the word. ✔

> **To Correct**
> 1. Say the sounds in **if.** (Signal.) *iiifff.*
> 2. Say the sounds the hard way. (Signal.) *iii* (pause) *fff.*
> 3. Write the word **if.** ✔

b. (Repeat step *a* for **it.**)

EXERCISE 3

Children write on

a. You're going to write the word **on.** Listen. **On.** Saying the sounds in (pause) **on** the hard way. Get ready. (Signal for each sound as the children say:) *ooo* (pause) *nnn.* (The children are to pause two seconds between the sounds.)

• (Repeat until firm.)

b. Everybody, write the word (pause) **on.** ✔

EXERCISE 4

Children write at

You're going to write the word **at.** Think about the sounds in (pause) **at** and write the word. ✔

EXERCISE 5

Children write mat, ram

a. You're going to write the word **mat.** Listen. **Mat.** Saying the sounds in (pause) **mat** the hard way. Get ready. (Signal for each sound as the children say:) *mmm* (pause) *aaa* (pause) *t.* (The children are to pause two seconds between the sounds.)

• (Repeat until firm.)

b. Everybody, write the word (pause) **mat.** ✔

c. (Repeat steps *a* and *b* for **ram.**)

Spelling Lesson 26

WORD WRITING
EXERCISE 1

Children write an

You're going to write the word **an.** Think about the sounds in (pause) **an** and write the word. ✔

> **To Correct**
> 1. Say the sounds in **an.** (Signal.) *aannn.*
> 2. Say the sounds the hard way. (Signal.) *aaa* (pause) *nnn.*
> 3. Write the word **an.** ✔

EXERCISE 2

Children write **fan, ran**

a. You're going to write the word **fan.** Listen. **Fan.** Saying the sounds in (pause) **fan** the hard way. Get ready. (Signal for each sound as the children say:) *fff* (pause) *aaa* (pause) *nnn.* (The children are to pause two seconds between the sounds.)
 • (Repeat until firm.)
b. Everybody, write the word (pause) **fan.** ✔
c. (Repeat steps *a* and *b* for **ran.**)

EXERCISE 3

Children write **man, it**

a. You're going to write the word **man.** Think about the sounds in (pause) **man** and write the word. ✔
b. (Repeat step *a* for **it.**)

EXERCISE 4

Children write **fit, on**

a. You're going to write the word **fit.** Listen. **Fit.** Saying the sounds in (pause) **fit** the hard way. Get ready. (Signal for each sound as the children say:) *fff* (pause) *iii* (pause) *t.* (The children are to pause two seconds between the sounds.)
 • (Repeat until firm.)
b. Everybody, write the word (pause) **fit.** ✔
c. (Repeat steps *a* and *b* for **on.**)

SPELLING LESSON 27

WORD WRITING
EXERCISE 1

Children write **am, an, ran, fan, man**

a. You're going to write the word **am.** Think about the sounds in (pause) **am** and write the word. ✔

To Correct
1. Say the sounds in **am.** (Signal.) *aaammm.*
2. Say the sounds the hard way. (Signal.) *aaa* (pause) *mmm.*
3. Write the word **am.** ✔

b. (Repeat step *a* for the following words: **an, ran, fan, man.**)

EXERCISE 2

Children write **fit, ron**

a. You're going to write the word **fit.** Listen. **Fit.** Saying the sounds in (pause) **fit** the hard way. Get ready. (Signal for each sound as the children say:) *fff* (pause) *iii* (pause) *t.* (The children are to pause two seconds between the sounds.)
 • (Repeat until firm.)
b. Everybody, write the word (pause) **fit.** ✔
c. (Repeat steps *a* and *b* for **ron.**)

SPELLING LESSON 28

WORD WRITING
EXERCISE 1

Children write **an, man, on, ron**

a. You're going to write the word **an.** Think about the sounds in (pause) **an** and write the word. ✔

To Correct
1. Say the sounds in **an.** (Signal.) *aaannn.*
2. Say the sounds the hard way. (Signal.) *aaa* (pause) *nnn.*
3. Write the word **an.** ✔

b. (Repeat step *a* for **man, on,** and **ron.**)

EXERCISE 2

Children write **mat**

a. You're going to write the word **mat.** Listen. **Mat.** Saying the sounds in (pause) **mat** the hard way. Get ready. (Signal for each sound as the children say:) *mmm* (pause) *aaa* (pause) *t.* (The children are to pause two seconds between the sounds.)
 • (Repeat until firm.)
b. Everybody, write the word (pause) **mat.** ✔

EXERCISE 3

Children write **it, fit**

- a. You're going to write the word **it.** Think about the sounds in (pause) **it** and write the word. ✔
- b. (Repeat step *a* for **fit.**)

SPELLING LESSON 29

WORD WRITING

Children write **am, ram, in, fin, on, ron, it, fit**

- a. You're going to write the word **am.** Think about the sounds in (pause) **am** and write the word. ✔

To Correct

1. Say the sounds in **am.** (Signal.) *aaammm.*
2. Say the sounds the hard way. (Signal.) *aaa* (pause) *mmm.*
3. Write the word **am.** ✔

- b. (Repeat step *a* for the following words: **ram, in, fin, on, ron, it, fit.**)

SPELLING LESSON 30

WORD WRITING

Children write **in, fin, at, mat, an, man, on, ron**

- a. You're going to write the word **in.** Think about the sounds in (pause) **in** and write the word. ✔

To Correct

1. Say the sounds in **in.** (Signal.) *iiinnn.*
2. Say the sounds the hard way. (Signal.) *iii* (pause) *nnn.*
3. Write the word **in.** ✔

- b. (Repeat step *a* for the following words: **fin, at, mat, an, man, on, ron.**

SPELLING LESSON 31

SOUND WRITING
EXERCISE 1

Children write **s**

- a. You're going to write a sound.
- b. Here's the sound you're going to write. Listen. **sss.** What sound? (Signal.) *sss.*
- c. Write **sss.** ✔

EXERCISE 2

Children write **it, if, in, on, an, am, at**

- a. You're going to write the word **it.** Think about the sounds in (pause) **it** and write the word. ✔

To Correct

1. Say the sounds in **it.** (Signal.) *iiit.*
2. Say the sounds the hard way. (Signal.) *iii* (pause) *t.*
3. Write the word **it.** ✔

- b. (Repeat step *a* for the following words: **if, in, on, an, am, at.**)

SPELLING LESSON 32

SOUND WRITING
EXERCISE 1

Children write **s**

- a. You're going to write a sound.
- b. Here's the sound you're going to write. Listen. **sss.** What sound? (Signal.) *sss.*
- c. Write **sss.** ✔

EXERCISE 2

Children write **if, it, sit, at, sat, in, sin**

- a. You're going to write the word **if.** Think about the sounds in (pause) **if** and write the word. ✔

To Correct

1. Say the sounds in **if.** (Signal.) *iiifff.*
2. Say the sounds the hard way. (Signal.) *iii* (pause) *fff.*
3. Write the word **if.** ✔

b. (Repeat step *a* for the following words: **it, sit, at, sat, in, sin.**)

Spelling Lesson 33

WORD WRITING
EXERCISE 1

Children write **an, am, mat, if, it, in, sin**

a. You're going to write the word **an.** Think about the sounds in (pause) **an** and write the word. ✔

> **To Correct**
> 1. Say the sounds in **an.** (Signal.) *aaannn.*
> 2. Say the sounds the hard way. (Signal.) *aaa* (pause) *nnn.*
> 3. Write the word **an.** ✔

b. (Repeat step *a* for the following words: **am, mat, if, it, in, sin.**)

EXERCISE 2

Children write **is**

a. You're going to write the word (pause) **is.** When you write the word (pause) **is,** you write these sounds. **iii** (pause) **sss.**
b. Say the sounds you write for (pause) **is.** Get ready. (Signal for each sound as the children say:) *iii* (pause) *sss.* (The children are to pause two seconds between the sounds.)
• (Repeat until firm.)
c. Everybody, write the word (pause) **is.** ✔

Spelling Lesson 34

SOUND WRITING
EXERCISE 1

Children write **h**

a. You're going to write a sound.
b. Here's the sound you're going to write. Listen. **h.** What sound? (Signal.) *h.*
c. Write **h.** ✔

WORD WRITING
EXERCISE 2

Children write **am, ram**

a. You're going to write the word **am.** Think about the sounds in (pause) **am** and write the word. ✔

> **To Correct**
> 1. Say the sounds in **am.** (Signal.) *aaammm.*
> 2. Say the sounds the hard way. (Signal.) *aaa* (pause) *mmm.*
> 3. Write the word **am.** ✔

b. (Repeat step *a* for **ram.**)

EXERCISE 3

Children write **is**

a. You're going to write the word (pause) **is.** When you write the word (pause) **is,** you write these sounds. **iii** (pause) **sss.**
b. Say the sounds you write for (pause) **is.** Get ready. (Signal for each sound as the children say:) *iii* (pause) *sss.* (The children are to pause two seconds between the sounds.)
• (Repeat until firm.)
c. Everybody, write the word (pause) **is.** ✔

EXERCISE 4

Children write **if, an, on, it, at**

a. You're going to write the word **if.** Think about the sounds in (pause) **if** and write the word. ✔

> **To Correct**
> 1. Say the sounds in **if.** (Signal.) *iiifff.*
> 2. Say the sounds the hard way. (Signal.) *iii* (pause) *fff.*
> 3. Write the word **if.** ✔

b. (Repeat step *a* for the following words: **an, on, it, at.**)

SPELLING LESSON 35

SOUND WRITING
EXERCISE 1

Children write **h**

a. You're going to write a sound.
b. Here's the sound you're going to write. Listen. **h.** What sound? (Signal.) *h.*
c. Write **h.** ✔

WORD WRITING
EXERCISE 2

Children write **is**

a. You're going to write the word (pause) **is.** When you write the word (pause) **is,** you write these sounds. **iii** (pause) **sss.**
b. Say the sounds you write for (pause) **is.** Get ready. (Signal for each sound as the children say:) *iii* (pause) *sss.* (The children are to pause two seconds between the sounds.)
• (Repeat until firm.)
c. Everybody, write the word (pause) **is.** ✔

EXERCISE 3

Children write **at, sat, it, sit, in, sin**

a. You're going to write the word **at.** Think about the sounds in (pause) **at** and write the word. ✔

> **To Correct**
> 1. Say the sounds in **at.** (Signal.) *aaat.*
> 2. Say the sounds the hard way. (Signal.) *aaa* (pause) *t.*
> 3. Write the word **at.** ✔

b. (Repeat step *a* for the following words: **sat, it, sit, in, sin.**)

SPELLING LESSON 36

WORD WRITING
EXERCISE 1

Children write **it, sit**

a. You're going to write the word **it.** Think about the sounds in (pause) **it** and write the word. ✔

> **To Correct**
> 1. Say the sounds in **it.** (Signal.) *iiit.*
> 2. Say the sounds the hard way. (Signal.) *iii* (pause) *t.*
> 3. Write the word **it.** ✔

b. (Repeat step *a* for **sit.**)

EXERCISE 2

Children write **hit**

a. You're going to write the word (pause) **hit.** This word is tough. I'll say the sounds in (pause) **hit** the hard way. Listen. **H** (pause one second) **iii** (pause one second) **t.**
b. Your turn. Say the sounds in (pause) **hit.** Get ready. (Signal for each sound as the children say:) *h* (pause) *iii* (pause) *t.* (The children are to pause two seconds between the sounds.)
• (Repeat until firm.)
c. Everybody, write the word (pause) **hit.** ✔

EXERCISE 3

Children write **at, fat, rat**

a. You're going to write the word **at.** Think about the sounds in (pause) **at** and write the word. ✔
b. (Repeat step *a* for **fat** and **rat.**)

EXERCISE 4

Children write **hat**

a. You're going to write the word (pause) **hat.** This word is tough. I'll say the sounds in (pause) **hat** the hard way. Listen. **H** (pause one second) **aaa** (pause one second) **t.**
b. Your turn. Say the sounds in (pause) **hat.** Get ready. (Signal for each sound as the children say:) *h* (pause) *aaa* (pause) *t.* (The children are to pause two seconds between sounds.)
• (Repeat until firm.)
c. Everybody, write the word (pause) **hat.** ✔

EXERCISE 5

Children write **is**

  a. You're going to write the word (pause) **is.** When you write the word (pause) **is,** you write these sounds. **iii** (pause) **sss.**

  b. Say the sounds you write for (pause) **is.** Get ready. (Signal for each sound as the children say:) *iii* (pause) *sss.* (The children are to pause two seconds between the sounds.)

  • (Repeat until firm.)

  c. Everybody, write the word (pause) **is.** ✔

SPELLING LESSON 37

WORD WRITING
EXERCISE 1

Children write **am, sam**

  a. You're going to write the word **am.** Think about the sounds in (pause) **am** and write the word. ✔

  ┌─── **To Correct** ─────────────
  1. Say the sounds in **am.** (Signal.) *aaammm.*
  2. Say the sounds the hard way. (Signal.) *aaa* (pause) *mmm.*
  3. Write the word **am.** ✔
  └────────────────────────────

  b. (Repeat step *a* for **sam.**)

EXERCISE 2

Children write **ham**

  a. You're going to write the word (pause) **ham.** This word is tough. I'll say the sounds in (pause) **ham** the hard way. Listen. **H** (pause one second) **aaa** (pause one second) **mmm.**

  b. Your turn. Say the sounds in (pause) **ham.** Get ready. (Signal for each sound as the children say:) *h* (pause) *aaa* (pause) *mmm.* (The children are to pause two seconds between the sounds.)

  • (Repeat until firm.)

  c. Everybody, write the word (pause) **ham.** ✔

EXERCISE 3

Children write **it**

You're going to write the word **it.** Think about the sounds in (pause) **it** and write the word. ✔

EXERCISE 4

Children write **hit**

  a. You're going to write the word (pause) **hit.** This word is tough. I'll say the sounds in (pause) **hit** the hard way. Listen. **H** (pause one second) **iii** (pause one second) **t.**

  b. Your turn. Say the sounds in (pause) **hit.** Get ready. (Signal for each sound as the children say:) *h* (pause) *iii* (pause) *t.* (The children are to pause two seconds between the sounds.)

  • (Repeat until firm.)

  c. Everybody, write the word (pause) **hit.** ✔

EXERCISE 5

Children write **an, fan**

  a. You're going to write the word **an.** Think about the sounds in (pause) **an** and write the word. ✔

  b. (Repeat step *a* for **fan.**)

EXERCISE 6

Children write **is**

  a. You're going to write the word (pause) **is.** Say the sounds you write for (pause) **is.** Get ready. (Signal for each sound as the children say:) *iii* (pause) *sss.* (The children are to pause two seconds between the sounds.)

  • (Repeat until firm.)

  b. Everybody, write the word (pause) **is.** ✔

SPELLING LESSON 38

WORD WRITING
EXERCISE 1

Children write **am**

You're going to write the word **am.** Think about the sounds in (pause) **am** and write the word. ✔

To Correct

1. Say the sounds in **am.** (Signal.) *aaammm.*
2. Say the sounds the hard way. (Signal.) *aaa* (pause) *mmm.*
3. Write the word **am.** ✔

EXERCISE 2

Children write **ham**

a. You're going to write the word (pause) **ham.** This word is tough. I'll say the sounds in (pause) **ham** the hard way. Listen. **H** (pause one second) **aaa** (pause one second) **mmm.**

b. Your turn. Say the sounds in (pause) **ham.** Get ready. (Signal for each sound as the children say:) *h* (pause) *aaa* (pause) *mmm.* (The children are to pause two seconds between the sounds.)

• (Repeat until firm.)

c. Everybody, write the word (pause) **ham.** ✔

EXERCISE 3

Children write **it**

You're going to write the word **it.** Think about the sounds in (pause) **it** and write the word. ✔

EXERCISE 4

Children write **hit**

a. Now you're going to write the word (pause) **hit.** This word is tough. I'll say the sounds in (pause) **hit** the hard way. Listen. **H** (pause one second) **iii** (pause one second) **t.**

b. Your turn. Say the sounds in (pause) **hit.** Get ready. (Signal for each sound as the children say:) *h* (pause) *iii* (pause) *t.* (The children are to pause two seconds between the sounds.)

• (Repeat until firm.)

c. Everybody, write the word (pause) **hit.** ✔

EXERCISE 5

Children write **is**

a. Everybody, you're going to write the word (pause) **is.** Say the sounds you write for (pause) **is.** Get ready. (Signal for each sound as the children say:) *iii* (pause) *sss.* (The children are to pause two seconds between the sounds.)

• (Repeat until firm.)

b. Everybody, write the word (pause) **is.** ✔

EXERCISE 6

Children write **his, has**

a. You're going to write the word (pause) **his.** When you write the word (pause) **his,** you write these sounds: **H** (pause) **iii** (pause) **sss.**

b. Say the sounds you write for (pause) **his.** Get ready. (Signal for each sound as the children say:) *h* (pause) *iii* (pause) *sss.* (The children are to pause two seconds between the sounds.)

• (Repeat until firm.)

c. Everybody, write the word (pause) **his.** ✔

d. You're going to write the word (pause) **has.** When you write the word (pause) **has,** you write these sounds: **H** (pause) **aaa** (pause) **sss.**

e. Say the sounds you write for (pause) **has.** (Signal for each sound as the children say:) *h* (pause) *aaa* (pause) *sss.* (The children are to pause two seconds between the sounds.)

• (Repeat until firm.)

f. Everybody, write the word (pause) **has.** ✔

EXERCISE 7

Children write **on**

You're going to write the word **on.** Think about the sounds in (pause) **on** and write the word. ✔

SPELLING LESSON 39

WORD WRITING
EXERCISE 1

Children write at

You're going to write the word **at.** Think about the sounds in (pause) **at** and write the word. ✔

> **To Correct**
> 1. Say the sounds in **at.** (Signal.) *aaat.*
> 2. Say the sounds the hard way. (Signal.) *aaa* (pause) *t.*
> 3. Write the word **at.** ✔

EXERCISE 2

Children write hat

a. You're going to write the word (pause) **hat.** This word is tough. I'll say the sounds in (pause) **hat** the hard way. Listen. **H** (pause) **aaa** (pause) **t.**

b. Your turn. Say the sounds in (pause) **hat.** Get ready. (Signal for each sound as the children say:) *h* (pause) *aaa* (pause) *t.* (The children are to pause two seconds between the sounds.)

• (Repeat until firm.)

c. Everybody, write the word (pause) **hat.** ✔

EXERCISE 3

Children write it

You're going to write the word **it.** Think about the sounds in (pause) **it** and write the word. ✔

EXERCISE 4

Children write hit

a. You're going to write the word (pause) **hit.** This word is tough. I'll say the sounds in (pause) **hit** the hard way. Listen. **H** (pause) **iii** (pause) **t.**

b. Your turn. Say the sounds in (pause) **hit.** Get ready. (Signal for each sound as the children say:) *h* (pause) *iii* (pause) *t.* (The children are to pause two seconds between the sounds.)

• (Repeat until firm.)

c. Everybody, write the word (pause) **hit.** ✔

EXERCISE 5

Children write is, his

a. You're going to write the word (pause) **is.** Say the sounds you write for (pause) **is.** Get ready. (Signal for each sound as the children say:) *iii* (pause) *sss.* (The children are to pause two seconds between the sounds.)

• (Repeat until firm.)

b. Everybody, write the word (pause) **is.** ✔

c. Now, you're going to write the word (pause) **his.** Say the sounds you write for (pause) **his.** Get ready. (Signal for each sound as the children say:) *h* (pause) *iii* (pause) *sss.* (The children are to pause two seconds between the sounds.)

• (Repeat until firm.)

d. Everybody, write the word (pause) **his.** ✔

EXERCISE 6

Children write has

a. You're going to write the word (pause) **has.** When you write the word (pause) **has,** you write these sounds. **H** (pause) **aaa** (pause) **sss.**

b. Say the sounds you write for (pause) **has.** Get ready. (Signal for each sound as the children say:) *h* (pause) *aaa* (pause) *sss.* (The children are to pause two seconds between the sounds.)

• (Repeat until firm.)

c. Everybody, write the word (pause) **has.** ✔

EXERCISE 7

Children write ham

a. You're going to write the word (pause) **ham.** This word is tough. I'll say the sounds in (pause) **ham** the hard way. Listen. **H** (pause) **aaa** (pause) **mmm.**

b. Your turn. Say the sounds in (pause) **ham.** Get ready. (Signal for each sound as the children say:) *h* (pause) *aaa* (pause) *mmm.* (The children are to pause two seconds between the sounds.)

• (Repeat until firm.)

c. Everybody, write the word (pause) **ham.** ✔

SPELLING LESSON 40

WORD WRITING
EXERCISE 1

Children write **not, rot**

a. You're going to write the word **not.**
   Listen. **Not.** Saying the sounds in
   (pause) **not** the hard way. Get ready.
   (Signal for each sound as the children
   say:) *nnn* (pause) *ooo* (pause) *t.* (The
   children are to pause two seconds
   between the sounds.)
- (Repeat until firm.)

b. Everybody, write the word (pause) **not.** ✔

c. (Repeat steps *a* and *b* for **rot.**)

EXERCISE 2

Children write **hot**

a. You're going to write the word (pause)
   hot. This word is tough. I'll say the
   sounds in (pause) **hot** the hard way.
   Listen. **H** (pause) **ooo** (pause) **t.**

b. Your turn. Say the sounds in (pause) **hot.**
   Get ready. (Signal for each sound as the
   children say:) *h* (pause) *ooo* (pause) *t.*
   (The children are to pause two seconds
   between the sounds.)
- (Repeat until firm.)

c. Everybody, write the word (pause) **hot.** ✔

EXERCISE 3

Children write **rat, fat**

a. You're going to write the word **rat.**
   Think about the sounds in (pause) **rat**
   and write the word. ✔

> **To Correct**
> 1. Say the sounds in **rat.** (Signal.) *rrraaat.*
> 2. Say the sounds the hard way. (Signal.)
>   *rrr* (pause) *aaa* (pause) *t.*
> 3. Write the word **rat.** ✔

b. (Repeat step *a* for **fat.**)

EXERCISE 4

Children write **hat**

a. You're going to write the word (pause)
   hat. This word is tough. I'll say the
   sounds in (pause) **hat** the hard way.
   Listen. **H** (pause) **aaa** (pause) **t.**

b. Your turn. Say the sounds in (pause) **hat.**
   Get ready. (Signal for each sound as the
   children say:) *h* (pause) *aaa* (pause) *t.*
   (The children are to pause two seconds
   between the sounds.)
- (Repeat until firm.)

c. Everybody, write the word (pause) **hat.** ✔

EXERCISE 5

Children write **is, his**

a. You're going to write the word (pause)
   is. Say the sounds you write for (pause)
   is. Get ready. (Signal for each sound as
   the children say:) *iii* (pause) *sss.* (The
   children are to pause two seconds
   between the sounds.)
- (Repeat until firm.)

b. Everybody, write the word (pause) **is.** ✔

c. Now, you're going to write the word (pause)
   his. Say the sounds you write for (pause)
   his. Get ready. (Signal for each sound as
   the children say:) *h* (pause) *iii* (pause) *sss.*
   (The children are to pause two seconds
   between the sounds.)
- (Repeat until firm.)

d. Everybody, write the word (pause) **his.** ✔

SPELLING LESSON 41

WORD WRITING
EXERCISE 1

Children write **hat, hot**

a. You're going to write the word (pause)
   hat. This word is tough. I'll say the
   sounds in (pause) **hat** the hard way.
   Listen. **H** (pause) **aaa** (pause) **t.**

b. Your turn. Say the sounds in (pause)
   hat. Get ready. (Signal for each sound
   as the children say:) *h* (pause) *aaa*
   (pause) *t.* (The children are to pause two
   seconds between the sounds.)

- (Repeat until firm.)
c. Everybody, write the word (pause) **hat.** ✔
d. Now, you're going to write the word (pause) **hot.** This word is tough. I'll say the sounds in (pause) **hot** the hard way. Listen. **H** (pause) **ooo** (pause) **t.**
e. Your turn. Say the sounds in (pause) **hot.** Get ready. (Signal for each sound as the children say:) *h* (pause) *ooo* (pause) *t.* (The children are to pause two seconds between the sounds.)
- (Repeat until firm.)
f. Everybody, write the word (pause) **hot.** ✔

EXERCISE 2

Children write hit, ham

a. You're going to write the word **hit.** Think about the sounds in (pause) **hit** and write the word. ✔

To Correct ─────
1. Say the sounds in **hit.** (Signal.) *hiiit.*
2. Say the sounds the hard way. (Signal.) *h* (pause) *iii* (pause) *t.*
3. Write the word **hit.** ✔

b. (Repeat step *a* for **ham.**)

EXERCISE 3

Children write has

a. You're going to write the word (pause) **has.** Say the sounds you write for (pause) **has.** Get ready. (Signal for each sound as the children say:) *h* (pause) *aaa* (pause) *sss.* (The children are to pause two seconds between the sounds.)
- (Repeat until firm.)
b. Everybody, write the word (pause) **has.** ✔

EXERCISE 4

Children write sat, sit, not

a. You're going to write the word **sat.** Think about the sounds in (pause) **sat** and write the word. ✔
b. (Repeat step *a* for **sit** and **not.**)

SPELLING LESSON 42

WORD WRITING
EXERCISE 1

Children write at, is, on, not, if

a. You're going to write the word **at.** Think about the sounds in (pause) **at** and write the word. ✔

To Correct ─────
1. Say the sounds in **at.** (Signal.) *aaat.*
2. Say the sounds the hard way. (Signal.) *aaa* (pause) *t.*
3. Write the word **at.** ✔

b. You're going to write the word **is.** Think about the sounds in (pause) **is** and write the word. ✔

To Correct ─────
1. Say the sounds the hard way. (Signal.) *iii* (pause) *sss.*
2. Write the word **is.** ✔

c. (Repeat step *a* for **on, not,** and **if.**)

EXERCISE 2

Children write hot

a. You're going to write the word (pause) **hot.** This word is tough. I'll say the sounds in (pause) **hot** the hard way. Listen. **H** (pause) **ooo** (pause) **t.**
b. Your turn. Say the sounds in (pause) **hot.** Get ready. (Signal for each sound as the children say:) *h* (pause) *ooo* (pause) *t.* (The children are to pause two seconds between the sounds.)
- (Repeat until firm.)
c. Everybody, write the word (pause) **hot.** ✔

EXERCISE 3

Children write rim

a. You're going to write the word **rim.** Listen. **Rim.** Saying the sounds in (pause) **rim** the hard way. Get ready. (Signal for each sound as the children say:) *rrr* (pause) *iii* (pause) *mmm.* (The children are to pause two seconds between the sounds.)

- (Repeat until firm.)

b. Everybody, write the word (pause) **rim.** ✔

EXERCISE 4

Children write him

a. You're going to write the word (pause) **him.** This word is tough. I'll say the sounds in (pause) **him** the hard way. Listen. **H** (pause) **iii** (pause) **mmm.**

b. Your turn. Say the sounds in (pause) **him.** Get ready. (Signal for each sound as the children say:) *h* (pause) *iii* (pause) *mmm.* (The children are to pause two seconds between the sounds.)

- (Repeat until firm.)

c. Everybody, write the word (pause) **him.** ✔

SPELLING LESSON 43

SOUND WRITING
EXERCISE 1

Children write u

a. You're going to write a sound.

b. Here's the sound you're going to write. Listen. **uuu.** What sound? (Signal.) *uuu.*

c. Write **uuu.** ✔

WORD WRITING
EXERCISE 2

Children write sam, ham, not, hit, hat

a. You're going to write the word **sam.** Think about the sounds in (pause) **sam** and write the word. ✔

b. (Repeat step *a* for the following: **ham, not, hit, hat.**)

To Correct

1. Say the sounds in **sam.** (Signal.) *sssaaammm.*
2. Say the sounds the hard way. (Signal.) *sss* (pause) *aaa* (pause) *mmm.*
3. Write the word **sam.** ✔

EXERCISE 3

Children write him

a. You're going to write the word (pause) **him.** This word is tough. I'll say the sounds in (pause) **him** the hard way. Listen. **H** (pause) **iii** (pause) **mmm.**

b. Your turn. Say the sounds in (pause) **him.** Get ready. (Signal for each sound as the children say:) *h* (pause) *iii* (pause) *mmm.* (The children are to pause two seconds between the sounds.)

- (Repeat until firm.)

c. Everybody, write the word (pause) **him.** ✔

EXERCISE 4

Children write on, if

a. You're going to write the word **on.** Think about the sounds in (pause) **on** and write the word. ✔

b. (Repeat step *a* for **if.**)

SPELLING LESSON 44

SOUND WRITING
EXERCISE 1

Children write u

a. You're going to write a sound.

b. Here's the sound you're going to write. Listen. **uuu.** What sound? (Signal.) *uuu.*

c. Write **uuu.** ✔

WORD WRITING
EXERCISE 2

Children write him

a. You're going to write the word (pause) **him.** This word is tough.

- I'll say the sounds in (pause) **him** the hard way. Listen. **H** (pause) **iii** (pause) **mmm.**
  b. Your turn. Say the sounds in (pause) **him.** Get ready. (Signal for each sound as the children say:) *h* (pause) *iii* (pause) *mmm.* (The children are to pause two seconds between the sounds.)
- (Repeat until firm.)
  c. Everybody, write the word (pause) **him.**

EXERCISE 3

Children write **sun**

a. You're going to write the word **sun.** Listen. **Sun.** Say the sounds in (pause) **sun** the hard way. Get ready. (Signal for each sound as the children say:) *sss* (pause) *uuu* (pause) *nnn.* (The children are to pause two seconds between the sounds.)
- (Repeat until firm.)
b. Everybody, write the word (pause) **sun.** ✔

EXERCISE 4

Children write **not**

You're going to write the word **not.** Think about the sounds in (pause) **not** and write the word. ✔

> ### To Correct
> 1. Say the sounds in **not.** (Signal.) *nnnooot.*
> 2. Say the sounds the hard way. (Signal.) *nnn* (pause) *ooo* (pause) *t.*
> 3. Write the word **not.** ✔

EXERCISE 5

Children write **nut**

a. You're going to write the word **nut.** Listen. **Nut.** Saying the sounds in (pause) **nut** the hard way. Get ready. (Signal for each sound as the children say:) *nnn* (pause) *uuu* (pause) *t.* (The children are to pause two seconds between the sounds.)
- (Repeat until firm.)
b. Everybody, write the word (pause) **nut.** ✔

EXERCISE 6

Children write **ron**

You're going to write the word **ron.** Think about the sounds in (pause) **ron** and write the word. ✔

EXERCISE 7

Children write **run, fun**

a. You're going to write the word **run.** Listen. **Run.** Saying the sounds in (pause) **run** the hard way. Get ready. (Signal for each sound as the children say:) *rrr* (pause) *uuu* (pause) *nnn.* (The children are to pause two seconds between the sounds.)
- (Repeat until firm.)
b. Everybody, write the word (pause) **run.** ✔
c. (Repeat steps *a* and *b* for **fun.**)

EXERCISE 8

Children write **if**

You're going to write the word **if.** Think about the sounds in (pause) **if** and write the word. ✔

SPELLING LESSON 45

WORD WRITING
EXERCISE 1

Children write **fun**

a. You're going to write the word **fun.** Listen. **Fun.** Saying the sounds in (pause) **fun** the hard way. Get ready. (Signal for each sound as the children say:) *fff* (pause) *uuu* (pause) *nnn.* (The children are to pause two seconds between the sounds.)
- (Repeat until firm.)
b. Everybody, write the word (pause) **fun.** ✔

EXERCISE 2

Children write **fin, on, am**

a. You're going to write the word **fin.** Think about the sounds in (pause) **fin** and write the word. ✔

To Correct

1. Say the sounds in **fin**. (Signal.) *ffffiiinnn.*
2. Say the sounds the hard way. (Signal.) *fff* (pause) *iii* (pause) *nnn.*
3. Write the word **fin.** ✔

b. (Repeat step *a* for **on** and **am.**)

EXERCISE 3

Children write **his**

a. You're going to write the word (pause) **his.** Say the sounds you write for (pause) **his.** Get ready. (Signal for each sound as the children say:) *h* (pause) *iii* (pause) *sss.* (The children are to pause two seconds between the sounds.)

• (Repeat until firm.)

b. Everybody, write the word (pause) **his.** ✔

EXERCISE 4

Children write **hot**

You're going to write the word **hot.** Think about the sounds in (pause) **hot** and write the word. ✔

EXERCISE 5

Children write **nut**

a. You're going to write the word **nut.** Listen. **Nut.** Saying the sounds in (pause) **nut** the hard way. Get ready. (Signal for each sound as the children say:) *nnn* (pause) *uuu* (pause) *t.* (The children are to pause two seconds between the sounds.)

• (Repeat until firm.)

b. Everybody, write the word (pause) **nut.** ✔

SPELLING LESSON 46

WORD WRITING
EXERCISE 1

Children write **ran**

You're going to write the word **ran.** Think about the sounds in (pause) **ran** and write the word. ✔

To Correct

1. Say the sounds in **ran**. (Signal.) *rrraaannn.*
2. Say the sounds the hard way. (Signal.) *rrr* (pause) *aaa* (pause) *nnn.*
3. Write the word **ran.** ✔

EXERCISE 2

Children write **run**

a. You're going to write the word **run.** Listen. **Run.** Saying the sounds in (pause) **run** the hard way. Get ready. (Signal for each sound as the children say:) *rrr* (pause) *uuu* (pause) *nnn.* (The children are to pause two seconds between the sounds.)

• (Repeat until firm.)

b. Everybody, write the word (pause) **run.** ✔

EXERCISE 3

Children write **sit, sun, hot**

a. You're going to write the word **sit.** Think about the sounds in (pause) **sit** and write the word. ✔

b. (Repeat step *a* for **sun** and **hot.**)

EXERCISE 4

Children write **hut**

a. You're going to write the word **hut.** Listen. **Hut.** Saying the sounds in (pause) **hut** the hard way. Get ready. (Signal for each sound as the children say:) *h* (pause) *uuu* (pause) *t.* (The children are to pause two seconds between the sounds.)

• (Repeat until firm.)

b. Everybody, write the word (pause) **hut.** ✔

EXERCISE 5

Children write **hit**

You're going to write the word **hit.** Think about the sounds in (pause) **hit** and write the word. ✔

Spelling Lesson 47

WORD WRITING
EXERCISE 1

Children write **hum**

a. You're going to write the word (pause) **hum.** This word is tough. I'll say the sounds in (pause) **hum** the hard way. Listen. **H** (pause) **uuu** (pause) **mmm.**

b. Your turn. Say the sounds in (pause) **hum.** Get ready. (Signal for each sound as the children say:) *h* (pause) *uuu* (pause) *mmm.* (The children are to pause two seconds between the sounds.)

• (Repeat until firm.)

c. Everybody, write the word (pause) **hum.** ✔

EXERCISE 2

Children write **him, ham**

a. You're going to write the word **him.** Think about the sounds in (pause) **him** and write the word. ✔

> **To Correct**
> 1. Say the sounds in **him.** (Signal.) *hiiimmm.*
> 2. Say the sounds the hard way. (Signal.) *h* (pause) *iii* (pause) *mmm.*
> 3. Write the word **him.** ✔

b. (Repeat step *a* for **ham.**)

EXERCISE 3

Children write **has**

a. You're going to write the word (pause) **has.** Say the sounds you write for (pause) **has.** Get ready. (Signal for each sound as the children say:) *h* (pause) *aaa* (pause) *sss.* (The children are to pause two seconds between the sounds.)

• (Repeat until firm.)

b. Everybody, write the word (pause) **has.** ✔

EXERCISE 4

Children write **not, nut, rut, on**

a. You're going to write the word **not.** Think about the sounds in (pause) **not** and write the word. ✔

b. (Repeat step *a* for **nut, rut,** and **on.**)

Spelling Lesson 48

WORD WRITING

Children write **fit, on, rat, his, has, mat, run, sit**

a. You're going to write the word **fit.** Think about the sounds in (pause) **fit** and write the word. ✔

> **To Correct**
> 1. Say the sounds in **fit.** (Signal.) *fffiiit.*
> 2. Say the sounds the hard way. (Signal.) *fff* (pause) *iii* (pause) *t.*
> 3. Write the word **fit.** ✔

b. (Repeat step *a* for **on** and **rat.**)

c. You're going to write the word **his.** Think about the sounds in (pause) **his** and write the word. ✔

> **To Correct**
> 1. Say the sounds the hard way. (Signal.) *h* (pause) *iii* (pause) *sss.*
> 2. Write the word **his.** ✔

d. (Repeat step *c* for **has.**)

e. (Repeat step *a* for **mat, run,** and **sit.**)

Spelling Lesson 49

WORD WRITING

Children write **fat, run, is, fan, hut, hat, fun, hot**

a. You're going to write the word **fat.** Think about the sounds in (pause) **fat** and write the word. ✔

> **To Correct**
> 1. Say the sounds in **fat.** (Signal.) *fffaaat.*
> 2. Say the sounds the hard way. (Signal.) *fff* (pause) *aaa* (pause) *t.*
> 3. Write the word **fat.** ✔

b. (Repeat step *a* for **run, fan, hut, hat, fun, hot.**)

c. You're going to write the word **is.** Think about the sounds in (pause) **is** and write the word. ✔

> **To Correct**
> 1. Say the sounds the hard way. (Signal.) *iii* (pause) *sss.*
> 2. Write the word **is.** ✔

Spelling Lesson 50

WORD WRITING

Children write **fun, if, not, run, sit, ran, sat, fan**

a. You're going to write the word **fun.** Think about the sounds in (pause) **fun** and write the word. ✔

> **To Correct**
> 1. Say the sounds in **fun.** (Signal.) *fffuuunnn.*
> 2. Say the sounds the hard way. (Signal.) *fff* (pause) *uuu* (pause) *nnn.*
> 3. Write the word **fun.** ✔

b. (Repeat step *a* for the following: **if, not, run, sit, ran, sat, fan.**)

Spelling Lesson 51

WORD WRITING

Children write **ham, nut, fat, hot, fun, hit, on, has**

a. You're going to write the word **ham.** Think about the sounds in (pause) **ham** and write the word. ✔

> **To Correct**
> 1. Say the sounds in ham. (Signal.) *haaammm.*
> 2. Say the sounds the hard way. (Signal.) *h* (pause) *aaa* (pause) *mmm.*
> 3. Write the word **ham.** ✔

b. (Repeat step *a* for the following: **nut, fat, hot, fun, hit, on.**)

c. You're going to write the word **has.** Think about the sounds in (pause) **has** and write the word. ✔

> **To Correct**
> 1. Say the sounds the hard way. (Signal.) *h* (pause) *aaa* (pause) *sss.*
> 2. Write the word **has.** ✔

Spelling Lesson 52

WORD WRITING

Children write **rat, ran, fit, sun, rut, an, fin, hut**

a. You're going to write the word **rat.** Think about the sounds in (pause) **rat** and write the word. ✔

> **To Correct**
> 1. Say the sounds in **rat.** (Signal.) *rrraaat.*
> 2. Say the sounds the hard way. (Signal.) *rrr* (pause) *aaa* (pause) *t.*
> 3. Write the word **rat.** ✔

b. (Repeat step *a* for the following: **ran, fit, sun, rut, an, fin, hut.**)

Spelling Lesson 53

WORD WRITING

Children write **him, ham, hot, if, am, hum, not, on**

a. You're going to write the word **him.** Think about the sounds in (pause) **him** and write the word. ✔

b. (Repeat step *a* for the following: **ham, hot, if, am, hum, not, on.**)

To Correct _____

1. Say the sounds in **him.** (Signal.) *hiiimmm.*
2. Say the sounds the hard way. (Signal.) *h* (pause) *iii* (pause) *mmm.*
3. Write the word **him.** ✔

Spelling Lesson 54

SOUND WRITING
EXERCISE 1

Children write **d**

a. You're going to write a sound.
b. Here's the sound you're going to write. Listen. **d.** What sound? (Signal.) *d.*
c. Write **d.** ✔

WORD WRITING
EXERCISE 2

Children write **is, an, run, mat, in, rut, on, hat**

a. You're going to write the word **is.** Think about the sounds in (pause) **is** and write the word. ✔

To Correct _____

1. Say the sounds the hard way. (Signal.) *iii* (pause) *sss.*
2. Write the word **is.** ✔

b. You're going to write the word **an.** Think about the sounds in (pause) **an** and write the word. ✔

To Correct _____

1. Say the sounds in **an.** (Signal.) *aaannn.*
2. Say the sounds the hard way. (Signal.) *aaa* (pause) *nnn.*
3. Write the word **an.** ✔

c. (Repeat step *b* for the following: **run, mat, in, rut, on, hat.**)

Spelling Lesson 55

SOUND WRITING
EXERCISE 1

Children write **d**

a. You're going to write a sound.
b. Here's the sound you're going to write. Listen. **d.** What sound? (Signal.) *d.*
c. Write **d.** ✔

WORD WRITING
EXERCISE 2

Children write **has, mat**

a. You're going to write the word **has.** Think about the sounds in (pause) **has** and write the word. ✔

To Correct _____

1. Say the sounds the hard way. (Signal.) *h* (pause) *aaa* (pause) *sss.*
2. Write the word **has.** ✔

b. Now you're going to write the word **mat.** Think about the sounds in (pause) **mat** and write the word. ✔

To Correct _____

1. Say the sounds in **mat.** (Signal.) *mmmaaat.*
2. Say the sounds the hard way. (Signal.) *mmm* (pause) *aaa* (pause) *t.*
3. Write the word **mat.** ✔

EXERCISE 3

Children write **mad**

a. You're going to write the word **mad.** Listen. **Mad.** Saying the sounds in (pause) **mad** the hard way. Get ready. (Signal for each sound as the children say:) *mmm* (pause) *aaa* (pause) *d.* (The children are to pause two seconds between the sounds.)
• (Repeat until firm.)
b. Everybody, write the word (pause) **mad.** ✔

EXERCISE 4

Children write if

You're going to write the word **if.** Think about the sounds in (pause) **if** and write the word. ✔

EXERCISE 5

Children write sad

a. You're going to write the word **sad.** Listen. **Sad.** Saying the sounds in (pause) **sad** the hard way. Get ready. (Signal for each sound as the children say:) *sss* (pause) *aaa* (pause) *d.* (The children are to pause two seconds between the sounds.)
• (Repeat until firm.)
b. Everybody, write the word (pause) **sad.** ✔

EXERCISE 6

Children write had

a. You're going to write the word (pause) **had.** This word is tough. I'll say the sounds in (pause) **had** the hard way. Listen. **H** (pause one second) **aaa** (pause one second) **d.**
b. Your turn. Say the sounds in (pause) **had.** Get ready. (Signal for each sound as the children say:) *h* (pause) *aaa* (pause) *d.* (The children are to pause two seconds between the sounds.)
• (Repeat until firm.)
c. Everybody, write the word (pause) **had.** ✔

EXERCISE 7

Children write hot, nut

a. You're going to write the word **hot.** Think about the sounds in (pause) **hot** and write the word. ✔
b. (Repeat step *a* for **nut.**)

SPELLING LESSSON 56

WORD WRITING
EXERCISE 1

Children write mad, mud, sad

a. You're going to write the word **mad.** Listen. **Mad.** Saying the sounds in (pause) **mad** the hard way. Get ready. (Signal for each sound as the children say:) *mmm* (pause) *aaa* (pause) *d.* (The children are to pause two seconds between the sounds.)
• (Repeat until firm.)
b. Everybody, write the word (pause) **mad.** ✔
c. (Repeat steps *a* and *b* for **mud** and **sad.**)

EXERCISE 2

Children write mat, on

a. You're going to write the word **mat.** Think about the sounds in (pause) **mat** and write the word. ✔

To Correct _____

1. Say the sounds in **mat.** (Signal.) *mmmaaat.*
2. Say the sounds the hard way. (Signal.) *mmm* (pause) *aaa* (pause) *t.*
3. Write the word **mat.** ✔

b. (Repeat step *a* for **on.**)

EXERCISE 3

Children write had

a. You're going to write the word (pause) **had.** This word is tough. I'll say the sounds in (pause) **had** the hard way. Listen. **H** (pause one second) **aaa** (pause one second) **d.**
b. Your turn. Say the sounds in (pause) **had.** Get ready. (Signal for each sound as the children say:) *h* (pause) *aaa* (pause) *d.* (The children are to pause two seconds between the sounds.)
• (Repeat until firm.)
c. Everybody, write the word (pause) **had.** ✔

EXERCISE 4

Children write sit

You're going to write the word **sit.** Think about the sounds in (pause) **sit** and write the word. ✔

SPELLNG LESSON 57

WORD WRITING
EXERCISE 1

Children write hot, sad

a. You're going to write the word **hot.** Think about the sounds in (pause) **hot** and write the word. ✔

> **To Correct** _____
>
> 1. Say the sounds in **hot.** (Signal.) *hooot.*
> 2. Say the sounds the hard way. (Signal.) *h* (pause) *ooo* (pause) *t.*
> 3. Write the word **hot.** ✔

b. (Repeat step *a* for **sad.**)

EXERCISE 2

Children write nod

a. You're going to write the word **nod.** Listen. **Nod.** Saying the sounds in (pause) **nod** the hard way. Get ready. (Signal for each sound as the children say:) *nnn* (pause) *ooo* (pause) *d.* (The children are to pause two seconds between the sounds.)
• (Repeat until firm.)
b. Everybody, write the word (pause) **nod.** ✔

EXERCISE 3

Children write hum, his, him, nut, has

a. You're going to write the word **hum.** Think about the sounds in (pause) **hum** and write the word. ✔
b. You're going to write the word **his.** Think about the sounds in (pause) **his** and write the word. ✔

> **To Correct** _____
>
> 1. Say the sounds the hard way. (Signal.) *h* (pause) *iii* (pause) *sss.*
> 2. Write the word **his.** ✔

c. (Repeat step *a* for **him** and **nut.**)
d. (Repeat step *b* for **has.**)

SPELLING LESSON 58

WORD WRITING
EXERCISE 1

Children write sad, sun

a. You're going to write the word **sad.** Think about the sounds in (pause) **sad** and write the word. ✔

> **To Correct** _____
>
> 1. Say the sounds in **sad.** (Signal.) *sssaaad.*
> 2. Say the sounds the hard way. (Signal.) *sss* (pause) *aaa* (pause) *d.*
> 3. Write the word **sad.** ✔

b. (Repeat step *a* for **sun.**)

EXERCISE 2

Children write rid

a. You're going to write the word **rid.** Listen. **Rid.** Saying the sounds in (pause) **rid** the hard way. Get ready. (Signal for each sound as the children say:) *rrr* (pause) *iii* (pause) *d.* (The children are to pause two seconds between the sounds.)
• (Repeat until firm.)
b. Everybody, write the word (pause) **rid.** ✔

EXERCISE 3

Children write run, mad, it, mud, sit

a. You're going to write the word **run.** Think about the sounds in (pause) **run** and write the word. ✔
b. (Repeat step *a* for the following: **mad, it, mud, sit.**)

Spelling Lesson 59

WORD WRITING
EXERCISE 1

Children write **an, ran**

a. You're going to write the word **an.** Think about the sounds in (pause) **an** and write the word. ✔

To Correct

1. Say the sounds in **an.** (Signal.) *aaannn.*
2. Say the sounds the hard way. (Signal.) *aaa* (pause) *nnn.*
3. Write the word **an.** ✔

b. (Repeat step *a* for **ran.**)

EXERCISE 2

Children write **dan, tan**

a. You're going to write the word (pause) **dan.** This word is tough. I'll say the sounds in (pause) **dan** the hard way. Listen. **D** (pause) **aaa** (pause) **nnn.**

b. Your turn. Say the sounds in (pause) **dan.** Get ready. (Signal for each sound as the children say:) *d* (pause) *aaa* (pause) *nnn.* (The children are to pause two seconds between sounds.)

• (Repeat until firm.)

c. Everybody, write the word (pause) **dan.** ✔

d. Now you're going to write the word (pause) **tan.** This word is tough. I'll say the sounds in (pause) **tan** the hard way. Listen. **T** (pause) **aaa** (pause) **nnn.**

e. Your turn. Say the sounds in (pause) **tan.** Get ready. (Signal for each sound as the children say:) *t* (pause) *aaa* (pause) *nnn.* (The children are to pause two seconds between sounds.)

• (Repeat until firm.)

f. Everybody, write the word (pause) **tan.** ✔

EXERCISE 3

Children write **sun, fin, nut, mud**

a. You're going to write the word **sun.** Think about the sounds in (pause) **sun** and write the word. ✔

b. (Repeat step *a* for **fin, nut,** and **mud.**)

Spelling Lesson 60

WORD WRITING
EXERCISE 1

Children write **mud**

You're going to write the word **mud.** Think about the sounds in (pause) **mud** and write the word. ✔

To Correct

1. Say the sounds in **mud.** (Signal.) *mmmuuud.*
2. Say the sounds the hard way. (Signal.) *mmm* (pause) *uuu* (pause) *d.*
3. Write the word **mud.** ✔

EXERCISE 2

Children write **tan**

a. You're going to write the word (pause) **tan.** This word is tough. I'll say the sounds in (pause) **tan** the hard way. Listen. **T** (pause) **aaa** (pause) **nnn.**

b. Your turn. Say the sounds in (pause) **tan.** Get ready. (Signal for each sound as the children say:) *t* (pause) *aaa* (pause) *nnn.* (The children are to pause two seconds between sounds.)

• (Repeat until firm.)

c. Everybody, write the word (pause) **tan.** ✔

EXERCISE 3

Children write **not, fin, hat, fat, his, him**

a. You're going to write the word **not.** Think about the sounds in (pause) **not** and write the word. ✔

b. (Repeat step *a* for **fin, hat,** and **fat.**)

c. You're going to write the word **his.** Think about the sounds in (pause) **his** and write the word. ✔

To Correct

1. Say the sounds the hard way. (Signal.) *h* (pause) *iii* (pause) *sss.*
2. Write the word **his.** ✔

d. (Repeat step *a* for **him.**)

SPELLING LESSON 61

SOUND WRITING
EXERCISE 1

Children write ē

a. You're going to write a sound.
b. Here's the sound you're going to write. Listen. ēēē. What sound? (Signal.) ēēē.
c. Write ēēē. ✔ (Accept e.)

WORD WRITING
EXERCISE 2

Children write **ron, an**

a. You're going to write the word **ron.** Think about the sounds in (pause) **ron** and write the word. ✔

> ### To Correct
> 1. Say the sounds in **ron.** (Signal.) *rrrooonnn.*
> 2. Say the sounds the hard way. (Signal.) *rrr* (pause) *ooo* (pause) *nnn.*
> 3. Write the word **ron.** ✔

b. (Repeat step *a* for **an.**)

EXERCISE 3

Children write **and**

a. You're going to write the word **and.** Listen. **And.** Saying the sounds in (pause) **and** the hard way. Get ready. (Signal for each sound as the children say:) *aaa* (pause) *nnn* (pause) *d.* (The children are to pause two seconds between the sounds.)
• (Repeat until firm.)
b. Everybody, write the word (pause) **and.** ✔

EXERCISE 4

Children write **hit**

You're going to write the word **hit.** Think about the sounds in (pause) **hit** and write the word. ✔

EXERCISE 5

Children write **tan**

a. You're going to write the word (pause) **tan.** This word is tough. I'll say the sounds in (pause) **tan** the hard way. Listen. **T** (pause) **aaa** (pause) **nnn.**
b. Your turn. Say the sounds in (pause) **tan.** Get ready. (Signal for each sound as the children say:) *t* (pause) *aaa* (pause) *nnn.* (The children are to pause two seconds between the sounds.)
• (Repeat until firm.)
c. Everybody, write the word (pause) **tan.** ✔

EXERCISE 6

Children write **sit, his**

a. You're going to write the word **sit.** Think about the sounds in (pause) **sit** and write the word. ✔
b. (Repeat step *a* for **his.**)

SPELLING LESSON 62

SOUND WRITING
EXERCISE 1

Children write ē

a. You're going to write a sound.
b. Here's the sound you're going to write. Listen. ēēē.
What sound? (Signal.) ēēē.
c. Write ēēē. ✔

WORD WRITING
EXERCISE 2

Children write **me**

a. You're going to write the word **me.** Listen. **Me.** Saying the sounds in (pause) **me** the hard way. Get ready. (Signal for each sound as the children say:) *mmm* (pause) *ēēē.* (The children are to pause two seconds between the sounds.)
• (Repeat until firm.)
b. Everybody, write the word (pause) **me.** ✔ (Accept **me.**)

EXERCISE 3

Children write he

a. You're going to write the word (pause) **he.** This word is tough. I'll say the sounds in (pause) **he** the hard way. Listen. **H** (pause one second) ēēē.

b. Your turn. Say the sounds in (pause) **he.** Get ready. (Signal for each sound as the children say:) *h* (pause) ēēē. (The children are to pause two seconds between the sounds.)

• (Repeat until firm.)

c. Everybody, write the word (pause) **he.** ✔

EXERCISE 4

Children write ham

You're going to write the word **ham.** Think about the sounds in (pause) **ham** and write the word. ✔

EXERCISE 5

Children write and

a. You're going to write the word **and.** Listen. **And.** Saying the sounds in (pause) **and** the hard way. Get ready. (Signal for each sound as the children say:) *aaa* (pause) *nnn* (pause) *d.* (The children are to pause two seconds between the sounds.)

• (Repeat until firm.)

b. Everybody, write the word (pause) **and.** ✔

EXERCISE 6

Children write hand

a. You're going to write the word (pause) **hand.** This word is tough. I'll say the sounds in (pause) **hand** the hard way. Listen. **H** (pause) **aaa** (pause) **nnn** (pause) **d.**

b. Your turn. Say the sounds in (pause) **hand.** Get ready. (Signal for each sound as the children say:) *h* (pause) *aaa* (pause) *nnn* (pause) *d.* (The children are to pause two seconds between sounds.)

• (Repeat until firm.)

c. Everybody, write the word (pause) **hand.** ✔

EXERCISE 7

Children write mud, fit

a. You're going to write the word **mud.** Think about the sounds in (pause) **mud** and write the word. ✔

b. (Repeat step *a* for **fit.**)

SPELLING LESSON 63

WORD WRITING
EXERCISE 1

Children write me

a. You're going to write the word **me.** Listen. **Me.** Saying the sounds in (pause) **me** the hard way. Get ready. (Signal for each sound as the children say:) *mmm* (pause) ēēē. (The children are to pause two seconds between the sounds.)

• (Repeat until firm.)

b. Everybody, write the word (pause) **me.** ✔

EXERCISE 2

Children write he

a. You're going to write the word (pause) **he.** This word is tough. I'll say the sounds in (pause) **he** the hard way. Listen. **H** (pause one second) ēēē.

b. Your turn. Say the sounds in (pause) **he.** Get ready. (Signal for each sound as the children say:) *h* (pause) ēēē. (The children are to pause two seconds between the sounds.)

• (Repeat until firm.)

c. Everybody, write the word (pause) **he.** ✔

EXERCISE 3

Children write tan, fit

a. You're going to write the word **tan.** Think about the sounds in (pause) **tan** and write the word. ✔

To Correct _____

1. Say the sounds in **tan.** (Signal.) *taaannn.*
2. Say the sounds the hard way. (Signal.) *t* (pause) *aaa* (pause) *nnn.*
3. Write the word **tan.** ✔

b. (Repeat step *a* for **fit.**)

EXERCISE 4

Children write **and**

a. You're going to write the word **and.** Listen. **And.** Saying the sounds in (pause) **and** the hard way. Get ready. (Signal for each sound as the children say:) *aaa* (pause) *nnn* (pause) *d.* (The children are to pause two seconds between the sounds.)
• (Repeat until firm.)
b. Everybody, write the word (pause) **and.** ✔

EXERCISE 5

Children write **hand**

a. You're going to write the word (pause) **hand.** This word is tough. I'll say the sounds in (pause) **hand** the hard way. Listen. **H** (pause) **aaa** (pause) **nnn** (pause) **d.**
b. Your turn. Say the sounds in (pause) **hand.** Get ready. (Signal for each sound as the children say:) *h* (pause) *aaa* (pause) *nnn* (pause) *d.* (The children are to pause two seconds between the sounds.)
• (Repeat until firm.)
c. Everybody, write the word (pause) **hand.** ✔

EXERCISE 6

Children write **fan, sin**

a. You're going to write the word **fan.** Think about the sounds in (pause) **fan** and write the word. ✔
b. (Repeat step *a* for **sin.**)

SPELLING LESSON 64

SOUND WRITING
EXERCISE 1

Children write **w**

a. You're going to write a sound.
b. Here's the sound you're going to write. Listen. **www.** What sound? (Signal.) *www.*
c. Write **www.** ✔

WORD WRITING
EXERCISE 2

Children write **he**

a. You're going to write the word **he.** Listen. **He.** Saying the sounds in (pause) **he** the hard way. Get ready. (Signal for each sound as the children say:) *h* (pause) *ēēē.* (The children are to pause two seconds between the sounds.)
• (Repeat until firm.)
b. Everybody, write the word (pause) **he.** ✔

EXERCISE 3

Children write **hand**

a. You're going to write the word (pause) **hand.** This word is tough. I'll say the sounds in (pause) **hand** the hard way. Listen. **H** (pause) **aaa** (pause) **nnn** (pause) **d.**
b. Your turn. Say the sounds in (pause) **hand.** Get ready. (Signal for each sound as the children say:) *h* (pause) *aaa* (pause) *nnn* (pause) *d.* (The children are to pause two seconds between the sounds.)
• (Repeat until firm.)
c. Everybody, write the word (pause) **hand.** ✔

EXERCISE 4

Children write **me**

a. You're going to write the word **me.** Listen. **Me.** Saying the sounds in (pause) **me** the hard way. Get ready. (Signal for each sound as the children say:) *mmm* (pause) *ēēē.* (The children are to pause two seconds between the sounds.)

- (Repeat until firm.)
b. Everybody, write the word (pause) **me.** ✔

EXERCISE 5

Children write **tan, dan, in**

a. You're going to write the word **tan.**
Think about the sounds in **tan** and write
the word. ✔

To Correct _____

1. Say the sounds in **tan.** (Signal.)
taaannn.
2. Say the sounds the hard way. (Signal.)
t (pause) *aaa* (pause) *nnn.*
3. Write the word **tan.** ✔

b. (Repeat step *a* for **dan** and **in.**)

EXERCISE 6

Children write **tin**

a. You're going to write the word (pause)
tin. This word is tough. I'll say the
sounds in (pause) **tin** the hard way.
Listen. **T** (pause) **iii** (pause) **nnn.**
b. Your turn. Say the sounds in (pause) **tin.**
Get ready. (Signal for each sound as the
children say:) *t* (pause) *iii* (pause) *nnn.*
(The children are to pause two seconds
between the sounds.)
- (Repeat until firm.)
c. Everybody, write the word (pause) **tin.** ✔

EXERCISE 7

Children write **has**

You're going to write the word **has.** Think
about the sounds in (pause) **has** and write
the word. ✔

To Correct _____

1. Say the sounds the hard way. (Signal.)
h (pause) *aaa* (pause) *sss.*
2. Write the word **has.** ✔

SPELLING LESSON 65

SOUND WRITING
EXERCISE 1

Children write **w**

a. You're going to write a sound.
b. Here's the sound you're going to write.
Listen. **www.** What sound? (Signal.) *www.*
c. Write **www.** ✔

WORD WRITING
EXERCISE 2

Children write **we, had**

a. You're going to write the word **we.**
Listen. **We.** Saying the sounds in
(pause) **we** the hard way. Get ready.
(Signal for each sound as the children
say:) *www* (pause) *ēēē.* (The children
are to pause two seconds between the
sounds.)
- (Repeat until firm.)
b. Everybody, write the word (pause) **we.** ✔
c. (Repeat steps *a* and *b* for **had.**)

EXERCISE 3

Children write **he**

You're going to write the word **he.** Think
about the sounds in (pause) **he** and write
the word. ✔

To Correct _____

1. Say the sounds in **he.** (Signal.) *H ēēē.*
2. Say the sounds the hard way. (Signal.)
H (pause) *ēēē.*
3. Write the word **he.** ✔

EXERCISE 4

Children write **win**

a. You're going to write the word **win.**
Listen. **Win.** Saying the sounds in
(pause) **win** the hard way. Get ready.
(Signal for each sound as the children
say:) *www* (pause) *iii* (pause) *nnn.* (The
children are to pause two seconds
between the sounds.)

- (Repeat until firm.)
b. Everybody, write the word (pause) **win.** ✔

EXERCISE 5

Children write **fit, if, on**

a. You're going to write the word **fit.** Think about the sounds in (pause) **fit** and write the word. ✔
b. (Repeat step *a* for **if** and **on.**)

SPELLING LESSON 66

WORD WRITING
EXERCISE 1

Children write **dan, on**

a. You're going to write the word **dan.** Think about the sounds in (pause) **dan** and write the word. ✔

To Correct _____

1. Say the sounds in **dan.** (Signal.) *daaannn.*
2. Say the sounds the hard way. (Signal.) *d* (pause) *aaa* (pause) *nnn.*
3. Write the word **dan.** ✔

b. (Repeat step *a* for **on.**)

EXERCISE 2

Children write **we**

a. You're going to write the word **we.** Listen. **We.** Saying the sounds in (pause) **we** the hard way. Get ready. (Signal for each sound as the children say:) *www* (pause) *ēēē.* (The children are to pause two seconds between the sounds.)
- (Repeat until firm.)
b. Everybody, write the word (pause) **we.** ✔

EXERCISE 3

Children write **in, sun, he, it, at**

a. You're going to write the word **in.** Think about the sounds in (pause) **in** and write the word. ✔
b. (Repeat step *a* for the following: **sun, he, it, at.**)

SPELLING LESSON 67

WORD WRITING

Children write **we, an, at, if, is, and, has, his**

a. You're going to write the word **we.** Think about the sounds in (pause) **we** and write the word. ✔

To Correct _____

1. Say the sounds in **we.** (Signal.) *www ēēē.*
2. Say the sounds the hard way. (Signal.) *www* (pause) *ēēē.*
3. Write the word **we.** ✔

b. (Repeat step *a* for **an, at,** and **if.**)
c. You're going to write the word **is.** Think about the sounds in (pause) **is** and write the word. ✔

To Correct _____

1. Say the sounds the hard way. (Signal.) *iii* (pause) *sss.*
2. Write the word **is.** ✔

d. (Repeat step *a* for **and.**)
e. (Repeat step *c* for **has** and **his.**)

SPELLING LESSON 68

SOUND WRITING
EXERCISE 1

Children write **l** as in **land.**

a. You're going to write a sound.
b. Here's the sound you're going to write. Listen. *lll.* What sound? (Signal.) *lll.*
c. Write *lll.* ✔

WORD WRITING
EXERCISE 2

Children write **he, tan, mad, we**

a. You're going to write the word **he.** Think about the sounds in (pause) **he** and write the word. ✔

To Correct _____

1. Say the sounds in **he.** (Signal.) *H ēēē.*
2. Say the sounds the hard way. (Signal.) *H* (pause) *ēēē.*
3. Write the word **he.** ✔

b. (Repeat step *a* for **tan, mad,** and **we.**)

EXERCISE 3

Children write **land**

a. You're going to write the word **land.**
Listen. **Land.** Saying the sounds in (pause) **land** the hard way. Get ready. (Signal for each sound as the children say:) *lll* (pause) *aaa* (pause) *nnn* (pause) *d.* (The children are to pause two seconds between the sounds.)
• (Repeat until firm.)
b. Everybody, write the word (pause) **land.** ✔

EXERCISE 4

Children write **has, mud**

a. You're going to write the word **has.** Think about the sounds in (pause) **has** and write the word. ✔

To Correct _____

1. Say the sounds the hard way. (Signal.) *h* (pause) *aaa* (pause) *sss.*
2. Write the word **has.** ✔

b. (Repeat step *a* for **mud.**)

SPELLING LESSON 69

SOUND WRITING
EXERCISE 1

Children write **l** as in **land**

a. You're going to write a sound.
b. Here's the sound you're going to write. Listen. **lll.** What sound? (Signal.) *lll.*
c. Write **lll.** ✔

WORD WRITING
EXERCISE 2

Children write **nod**

a. You're going to write the word **nod.** Listen. **Nod.** Saying the sounds in (pause) **nod** the hard way. Get ready. (Signal for each sound as the children say:) *nnn* (pause) *ooo* (pause) *d.* (The children are to pause two seconds between the sounds.)
• (Repeat until firm.)
b. Everybody, write the word (pause) **nod.** ✔

EXERCISE 3

Children write **and, hand, land**

a. You're going to write the word **and.** Think about the sounds in (pause) **and** and write the word. ✔

To Correct _____

1. Say the sounds in **and.** (Signal.) *aaannnd.*
2. Say the sounds the hard way. (Signal.) *aaa* (pause) *nnn* (pause) *d.*
3. Write the word **and.** ✔

b. (Repeat step *a* for **hand** and **land.**)

EXERCISE 4

Children write **rid, lid**

a. You're going to write the word **rid.** Listen. **Rid.** Saying the sounds in (pause) **rid** the hard way. Get ready. (Signal for each sound as the children say:) *rrr* (pause) *iii* (pause) *d.* (The children are to pause two seconds between the sounds.)
• (Repeat until firm.)
b. Everybody, write the word (pause) **rid.** ✔
c. (Repeat steps *a* and *b* for **lid.**)

EXERCISE 5

Children write **if**

You're going to write the word **if.** Think about the sounds in (pause) **if** and write the word. ✔

Spelling Lesson 70

WORD WRITING
EXERCISE 1

Children write **hand, we, land, me, has**

a. You're going to write the word **hand.** Think about the sounds in (pause) **hand** and write the word. ✔
b. (Repeat step *a* for **we, land,** and **me.**)
c. You're going to write the word **has.** Think about the sounds in (pause) **has** and write the word. ✔

> **To Correct**
>
> 1. Say the sounds the hard way. (Signal.) *h* (pause) *aaa* (pause) *sss.*
> 2. Write the word **has.** ✔

EXERCISE 2

Children write **win**

a. You're going to write the word **win.** Listen. **Win.** Saying the sounds in (pause) **win** the hard way. Get ready. (Signal for each sound as the children say:) *www* (pause) *iii* (pause) *nnn.* (The children are to pause two seconds between the sounds.)
• (Repeat until firm.)
b. Everybody, write the word (pause) **win.** ✔

EXERCISE 3

Children write **sit, lit**

a. You're going to write the word **sit.** Think about the sounds in (pause) **sit** and write the word. ✔
b. (Repeat step *a* for **lit.**)

Spelling Lesson 71

WORD WRITING

Children write **hot, hand, mud, tan, dan, nut, if, land**

a. You're going to write the word **hot.** Think about the sounds in (pause) **hot** and write the word. ✔

> **To Correct**
>
> 1. Say the sounds in **hot.** (Signal.) *hooot.*
> 2. Say the sounds the hard way. (Signal.) *h* (pause) *ooo* (pause) *t.*
> 3. Write the word **hot.** ✔

b. (Repeat step *a* for the following: **hand, mud, tan, dan, nut, if, land.**)

Spelling Lesson 72

WORD WRITING

Children write **nod, fit, tan, dan, fin, tin, his**

a. You're going to write the word **nod.** Think about the sounds in (pause) **nod** and write the word. ✔

> **To Correct**
>
> 1. Say the sounds in **nod.** (Signal.) *nnnoood.*
> 2. Say the sounds the hard way. (Signal.) *nnn* (pause) *ooo* (pause) *d.*
> 3. Write the word **nod.** ✔

b. (Repeat step *a* for the following: **fit, tan, dan, fin, tin.**)
c. You're going to write the word **his.** Think about the sounds in (pause) **his** and write the word. ✔

> **To Correct**
>
> 1. Say the sounds the hard way. (Signal.) *h* (pause) *iii* (pause) *sss.*
> 2. Write the word **his.** ✔

Spelling Lesson 73

WORD WRITING

Children write **did, rid, hid**

a. You're going to write the word **did.** Listen. **Did.** Saying the sounds in (pause) **did** the hard way. Get ready. (Signal for each sound as the children say:) *d* (pause) *iii* (pause) *d.* (The children are to pause two seconds between the sounds.)

- (Repeat until firm.)

b. Everybody, write the word (pause) **did.** ✔

c. (Repeat steps *a* and *b* for **rid** and **hid.**)

EXERCISE 2

Children write **sin, tin, hand**

a. You're going to write the word **sin.** Think about the sounds in (pause) **sin** and write the word. ✔

> **To Correct**
>
> 1. Say the sounds in **sin.** (Signal.) *sssiiinnn.*
> 2. Say the sounds the hard way. (Signal.) *sss* (pause) *iii* (pause) *nnn.*
> 3. Write the word **sin.** ✔

b. (Repeat step *a* for **tin** and **hand.**)

EXERCISE 3

Children write **sand**

a. You're going to write the word **sand.** Listen. **Sand.** Saying the sounds in (pause) **sand** the hard way. Get ready. (Signal for each sound as the children say:) *sss* (pause) *aaa* (pause) *nnn* (pause) *d.* (The children are to pause two seconds between the sounds.)

- (Repeat until firm.)

b. Everybody, write the word (pause) **sand.** ✔

SPELLING LESSON 74

WORD WRITING
EXERCISE 1

Children write **did, dad**

a. You're going to write **did.** Listen. **Did.** Saying the sounds in (pause) **did** the hard way. Get ready. (Signal for each sound as the children say:) *d* (pause) *iii* (pause) *d.* (The children are to pause two seconds between the sounds.)

- (Repeat until firm.)

b. Everybody, write the word (pause) **did.** ✔

c. (Repeat steps *a* and *b* for **dad.**)

EXERCISE 2

Children write **tin**

You're going to write the word **tin.** Think about the sounds in (pause) **tin** and write the word. ✔

> **To Correct**
>
> 1. Say the sounds in **tin.** (Signal.) *tiiinnn.*
> 2. Say the sounds the hard way. (Signal.) *t* (pause) *iii* (pause) *nnn.*
> 3. Write the word **tin.** ✔

EXERCISE 3

Children write **sand**

a. You're going to write the word **sand.** Listen. **Sand.** Saying the sounds in (pause) **sand** the hard way. Get ready. (Signal for each sound as the children say:) *sss* (pause) *aaa* (pause) *nnn* (pause) *d.* (The children are to pause two seconds between the sounds.)

- (Repeat until firm.)

b. Everybody, write the word (pause) **sand.** ✔

EXERCISE 4

Children write **not, me, his**

a. You're going to write the word **not.** Think about the sounds in (pause) **not** and write the word. ✔

> **To Correct**
>
> 1. Say the sounds in **not.** (Signal.) *nnnooot.*
> 2. Say the sounds the hard way. (Signal.) *nnn* (pause) *ooo* (pause) *t.*
> 3. Write the word **not.** ✔

b. (Repeat step *a* for **me.**)

c. You're going to write the word **his.** Think about the sounds in (pause) **his** and write the word. ✔

To Correct

1. Say the sounds the hard way. (Signal.) *h* (pause) *iii* (pause) *sss.*
2. Write the word **his.** ✔

SPELLING LESSON 75

WORD WRITING
EXERCISE 1

Children write **sun, sit, he, sad**

a. You're going to write the word **sun.** Think about the sounds in (pause) **sun** and write the word. ✔

To Correct

1. Say the sounds in **sun.** (Signal.) *sssuuunnn.*
2. Say the sounds the hard way. (Signal.) *sss* (pause) *uuu* (pause) *nnn.*
3. Write the word **sun.** ✔

b. (Repeat step *a* for **sit, he,** and **sad.**)

EXERCISE 2

Children write **dad**

a. You're going to write the word **dad.** Listen. **Dad.** Saying the sounds in (pause) **dad** the hard way. Get ready. (Signal for each sound as the children say:) *d* (pause) *aaa* (pause) *d.* (The children are to pause two seconds between the sounds.)
• (Repeat until firm.)
b. Everybody, write the word (pause) **dad.** ✔

EXERCISE 3

Children write **had, ron, fit**

a. You're going to write the word **had.** Think about the sounds in (pause) **had** and write the word. ✔
b. (Repeat step *a* for **ron** and **fit.**)

SPELLING LESSON 76

WORD WRITING
EXERCISE 1

Children write **did**

a. You're going to write the word **did.** Listen. **Did.** Saying the sounds in (pause) **did** the hard way. Get ready. (Signal for each sound as the children say:) *d* (pause) *iii* (pause) *d.* (The children are to pause two seconds between the sounds.)
• (Repeat until firm.)
b. Everybody, write the word (pause) **did.** ✔

EXERCISE 2

Children write **land, not**

a. You're going to write the word **land.** Think about the sounds in (pause) **land** and write the word. ✔

To Correct

1. Say the sounds in **land.** (Signal.) *lllaaannnd.*
2. Say the sounds the hard way. (Signal.) *lll* (pause) *aaa* (pause) *nnn* (pause) *d.*
3. Write the word **land.** ✔

b. (Repeat step *a* for **not.**)

EXERCISE 3

Children write **hid**

a. You're going to write the word **hid.** Listen. **Hid.** Saying the sounds in (pause) **hid** the hard way. Get ready. (Signal for each sound as the children say:) *h* (pause) *iii* (pause) *d.* (The children are to pause two seconds between the sounds.)
• (Repeat until firm.)
b. Everybody, write the word (pause) **hid.** ✔

EXERCISE 4

Children write **has, mud, hot, we**

a. You're going to write the word **has.** Think about the sounds in (pause) **has** and write the word. ✔

To Correct

1. Say the sounds the hard way. (Signal.) *h* (pause) *aaa* (pause) *sss.*
2. Write the word **has.** ✔

b. You're going to write the word **mud.** Think about the sounds in (pause) **mud** and write the word. ✔

To Correct

1. Say the sounds in **mud.** (Signal.) *mmmuuud.*
2. Say the sounds the hard way. (Signal.) *mmm* (pause) *uuu* (pause) *d.*
3. Write the word **mud.** ✔

c. (Repeat step *b* for **hot** and **we.**)

Spelling Lesson 77

WORD WRITING

Children write **and, land, sand, hand, if, has, is, on**

a. You're going to write the word **and.** Think about the sounds in (pause) **and** and write the word. ✔

To Correct

1. Say the sounds in **and.** (Signal.) *aaannnd.*
2. Say the sounds the hard way. (Signal.) *aaa* (pause) *nnn* (pause) *d.*
3. Write the word **and.** ✔

b. (Repeat step *a* for the following: **land, sand, hand, if.**)

c. You're going to write the word **has.** Think about the sounds in (pause) **has** and write the word. ✔

To Correct

1. Say the sounds the hard way. (Signal.) *h* (pause) *aaa* (pause) *sss.*
2. Write the word **has.** ✔

d. (Repeat step *c* for **is.**)
e. (Repeat step *a* for **on.**)

44

Spelling Lesson 78

WORD WRITING
EXERCISE 1

Children write **me**

You're going to write the word **me.** Think about the sounds in (pause) **me** and write the word. ✔

To Correct

1. Say the sounds in **me.** (Signal.) *mmmēēē.*
2. Say the sounds the hard way. (Signal.) *mmm* (pause) *ēēē.*
3. Write the word **me.** ✔

EXERCISE 2

Children write **win**

a. You're going to write the word **win.** Listen. **Win.** Saying the sounds in (pause) **win** the hard way. Get ready. (Signal for each sound as the children say:) *www* (pause) *iii* (pause) *nnn.* (The children are to pause two seconds between the sounds.)
• (Repeat until firm.)
b. Everybody, write the word (pause) **win.** ✔

EXERCISE 3

Children write **and**

You're going to write the word **and.** Think about the sounds in (pause) **and** and write the word. ✔

EXERCISE 4

Children write **ant**

a. You're going to write the word (pause) **ant.** Say the sounds you write for (pause) **ant.** Get ready. (Signal for each sound as the children say:) *aaa* (pause) *nnn* (pause) *t.* (The children are to pause two seconds between the sounds.)
• (Repeat until firm.)
b. Everybody, write the word (pause) **ant.** ✔

EXERCISE 5

Children write we, sit, he, fat

a. You're going to write the word **we.** Think about the sounds in (pause) **we** and write the word. ✔

b. (Repeat step *a* for **sit, he,** and **fat.**)

SPELLING LESSON 79

WORD WRITING
EXERCISE 1

Children write **me, has**

a. You're going to write the word **me.** Think about the sounds in (pause) **me** and write the word. ✔

> **To Correct**
> 1. Say the sounds in **me.** (Signal.) *mmmēēē.*
> 2. Say the sounds the hard way. (Signal.) *mmm* (pause) *ēēē.*
> 3. Write the word **me.** ✔

b. Now you're going to write the word **has.** Think about the sounds in (pause) **has** and write the word. ✔

> **To Correct**
> 1. Say the sounds the hard way. (Signal.) *h* (pause) *aaa* (pause) *sss.*
> 2. Write the word **has.** ✔

EXERCISE 2

Children write **was**

a. You're going to write the word (pause) **was.** When you write the word (pause) **was,** you write these sounds. **www** (pause) **aaa** (pause) **sss.**

b. Say the sounds you write for (pause) **was.** (Signal for each sound as the children say:) *www* (pause) *aaa* (pause) *sss.* (The children are to pause two seconds between the sounds.)

• (Repeat until firm.)

c. Everybody, write the word (pause) **was.** ✔

EXERCISE 3

Children write **we**

You're going to write the word **we.** Think about the sounds in (pause) **we** and write the word. ✔

EXERCISE 4

Children write **dad**

a. You're going to write the word **dad.** Listen. **Dad.** Saying the sounds in (pause) **dad** the hard way. Get ready. (Signal for each sound as the children say:) *d* (pause) *aaa* (pause) *d.* (The children are to pause two seconds between the sounds.)

• (Repeat until firm.)

b. Everybody, write the word (pause) **dad.** ✔

EXERCISE 5

Children write **tin, an, ant**

a. You're going to write the word **tin.** Think about the sounds in (pause) **tin** and write the word. ✔

> **To Correct**
> 1. Say the sounds in **tin.** (Signal.) *tiiinnn.*
> 2. Say the sounds the hard way. (Signal.) *t* (pause) *iii* (pause) *nnn.*
> 3. Write the word **tin.** ✔

b. (Repeat step *a* for **an** and **ant.**)

SPELLING LESSON 80

WORD WRITING
EXERCISE 1

Children write **we**

a. You're going to write the word **we.** Think about the sounds in (pause) **we** and write the word. ✔

To Correct

1. Say the sounds in **we.** (Signal.) *wwwēēē.*
2. Say the sounds the hard way. (Signal.) *www* (pause) *ēēē.*
3. Write the word **we.** ✔

b. Now you're going to write the word **has.** Think about the sounds in (pause) **has** and write the word. ✔

To Correct

1. Say the sounds the hard way. (Signal.) *h* (pause) *aaa* (pause) *sss.*
2. Write the word **has.** ✔

EXERCISE 2

Children write **was**

a. You're going to write the word (pause) **was.** When you write the word (pause) **was,** you write these sounds. **Www** (pause) **aaa** (pause) **sss.**

b. Say the sounds you write for (pause) **was.** (Signal for each sound as the children say:) *www* (pause) *aaa* (pause) *sss.* (The children are to pause two seconds between sounds.)

• (Repeat until firm.)

c. Everybody, write the word (pause) **was.** ✔

EXERCISE 3

Children write **tin, land, sand**

a. You're going to write the word **tin.** Think about the sounds in (pause) **tin** and write the word. ✔

b. (Repeat step *a* for **land** and **sand.**)

SPELLING LESSON 81

WORD WRITING
EXERCISE 1

Children write **has**

You're going to write the word **has.** Think about the sounds in (pause) **has** and write the word. ✔

To Correct

1. Say the sounds the hard way. (Signal.) *h* (pause) *aaa* (pause) *sss.*
2. Write the word **has.** ✔

EXERCISE 2

Children write **was**

a. You're going to write the word (pause) **was.** When you write the word (pause) **was,** you write these sounds. **Www** (pause) **aaa** (pause) **sss.**

b. Say the sounds you write for (pause) **was.** (Signal for each sound as the children say:) *www* (pause) *aaa* (pause) *sss.* (The children are to pause two seconds between sounds.)

• (Repeat until firm.)

c. Everybody, write the word (pause) **was.** ✔

EXERCISE 3

Children write **hid, did, dad, tin**

a. You're going to write the word **hid.** Think about the sounds in (pause) **hid** and write the word. ✔

To Correct

1. Say the sounds in **hid.** *hiiid.*
2. Say the sounds the hard way. *h* (pause) *iii* (pause) *d.*
3. Write the word **hid.** ✔

b. (Repeat step *a* for **did, dad,** and **tin.**)

SPELLING LESSON 82

WORD WRITING
EXERCISE 1

Children write **is, has, his**

a. You're going to write the word **is.** Think about the sounds in (pause) **is** and write the word. ✔

b. (Repeat step *a* for **has** and **his.**)

To Correct

1. Say the sounds the hard way. (Signal.) *iii* (pause) *sss.*
2. Write the word **is.** ✔

EXERCISE 2

Children write **was**

a. You're going to write the word (pause) **was.** Say the sounds you write for (pause) **was.** Get ready. (Signal for each sound as the children say:) *www* (pause) *aaa* (pause) *sss.* (The children are to pause two seconds between the sounds.)
- (Repeat until firm.)

b. Everybody, write the word (pause) **was.** ✔

★ SENTENCE WRITING

EXERCISE 3

Children write a sentence

a. Listen to this sentence. **He hit me.** Your turn. Say that sentence. Get ready. (Signal.) *He hit me.*

b. Now you're going to say it the slow way. Get ready. (Signal for each word as the children say:) *He* (pause) *hit* (pause) *me.*
- (Repeat until firm.)

c. Everybody, write the sentence. Spell each word the right way. (As you check children's responses, remind the children:) Don't forget to put a period at the end of your sentence.

SPELLING LESSON 83

SOUND WRITING
EXERCISE 1

Children write **c**

Note: The sound **c** is pronounced **k**. Do not say **kuuh**.

a. You're going to write a sound.
b. Here's the sound you're going to write. Listen. **k.** What sound? (Signal.) *k.*

c. (Write **c** on the board.) Here's the **k** you're going to write. (Then erase **c**.)
d. Write **k.** ✔

WORD WRITING
EXERCISE 2

Children write **was**

a. You're going to write the word (pause) **was.** Say the sounds you write for (pause) **was.** Get ready. (Signal for each sound as the children say:) *www* (pause) *aaa* (pause) *sss.* (The children are to pause two seconds between the sounds.)
- (Repeat until firm.)

b. Everybody, write the word (pause) **was.** ✔

EXERCISE 3

Children write **tin, did, we**

a. You're going to write the word **tin.** Think about the sounds in (pause) **tin** and write the word. ✔

To Correct

1. Say the sounds in **tin.** (Signal.) *tiiinnn.*
2. Say the sounds the hard way. (Signal.) *t* (pause) *iii* (pause) *nnn.*
3. Write the word **tin.** ✔

b. (Repeat step *a* for **did** and **we.**)

SENTENCE WRITING
EXERCISE 4

Children write a sentence

a. Listen to this sentence. **We had sand.** Your turn. Say that sentence. Get ready. (Signal.) *We had sand.*

b. Now you're going to say it the slow way. Get ready. (Signal for each word as the children say:) *We* (pause) *had* (pause) *sand.*
- (Repeat until firm.)

c. Everybody, write the sentence. Spell each word the right way. (As you check children's responses, remind the children:) Don't forget to put a period at the end of your sentence.

SPELLING LESSON 84

SOUND WRITING
EXERCISE 1

Children write c

a. You're going to write a sound.
b. Here's the sound you're going to write. Listen. **k.** What sound? (Signal.) *k.*
c. (Write **c** on the board.) Here's the **k** you're going to write. (Then erase **c.**)
d. Write **k.** ✔

WORD WRITING
EXERCISE 2

Children write can

a. You're going to write the word (pause) **can.** This word is tough. I'll say the sounds in (pause) **can** the hard way. Listen. **K** (pause) **aaa** (pause) **nnn.**
b. Your turn. Say the sounds in (pause) **can.** Get ready. (Signal for each sound as the children say:) *k* (pause) *aaa* (pause) *nnn.* (The children are to pause two seconds between sounds.)
• (Repeat until firm.)
c. Everybody, write the word (pause) **can.** ✔

EXERCISE 3

Children write has

You're going to write the word **has.** Think about the sounds in (pause) **has** and write the word. ✔

> **To Correct** —————————
> 1. Say the sounds the hard way. (Signal.) *h* (pause) *aaa* (pause) *sss.*
> 2. Write the word **has.** ✔

EXERCISE 4

Children write was

a. You're going to write the word (pause) **was.** Say the sounds you write for (pause) **was.** Get ready. (Signal for each sound as the children say:) *www* (pause) *aaa* (pause) *sss.* (The children are to pause two seconds between the sounds.)

• (Repeat until firm.)
b. Everybody, write the word (pause) **was.** ✔

EXERCISE 5

Children write land, nut

a. You're going to write the word **land.** Think about the sounds in (pause) **land** and write the word. ✔

> **To Correct** —————————
> 1. Say the sounds in **land.** (Signal.) *lllaaannnd.*
> 2. Say the sounds the hard way. (Signal.) *lll* (pause) *aaa* (pause) *nnn* (pause) *d.*
> 3. Write the word **land.** ✔

b. (Repeat step *a* for **nut.**)

SENTENCE WRITING
EXERCISE 6

Children write a sentence

a. Listen to this sentence. **He had fun.** Your turn. Say that sentence. Get ready. (Signal.) *He had fun.*
b. Now you're going to say it the slow way. Get ready. (Signal for each word as the children say:) *He* (pause) *had* (pause) *fun.*
• (Repeat until firm.)
c. Everybody, write the sentence. Spell each word the right way. (As you check children's responses, remind the children:) Don't forget to put a period at the end of your sentence.

SPELLING LESSON 85

WORD WRITING
EXERCISE 1

Children write can

a. You're going to write the word (pause) **can.** This word is tough. I'll say the sounds in (pause) **can** the hard way. Listen. **K** (pause) **aaa** (pause) **nnn.**
b. Your turn. Say the sounds in (pause) **can.** Get ready. (Signal for each sound as the children say:) *k* (pause) *aaa* (pause) *nnn.* (The children are to pause two seconds between the sounds.)

- (Repeat until firm.)
c. Everybody, write the word (pause) **can.** ✔

EXERCISE 2

Children write **arm**

a. You're going to write the word (pause) **arm.** When you write the word (pause) **arm,** you write these sounds. **Aaa** (pause) **rrr** (pause) **mmm.**
b. Say the sounds you write for (pause) **arm.** (Signal for each sound as the children say:) *aaa* (pause) *rrr* (pause) *mmm.* (The children are to pause two seconds between the sounds.)
- (Repeat until firm.)
c. Everybody, write the word (pause) **arm.** ✔

EXERCISE 3

Children write **sand, fit, mud, tin**

a. You're going to write the word **sand.** Think about the sounds in (pause) **sand** and write the word. ✔

To Correct

1. Say the sounds in **sand.** (Signal.) *sssaaannnd.*
2. Say the sounds the hard way. (Signal.) *sss* (pause) *aaa* (pause) *nnn* (pause) *d.*
3. Write the word **sand.** ✔

b. (Repeat step *a* for **fit, mud,** and **tin.**)

SENTENCE WRITING
EXERCISE 4

Children write a sentence

a. Listen to this sentence. **He was mad.** Your turn. Say that sentence. Get ready. (Signal.) *He was mad.*
b. Now you're going to say it the slow way. Get ready. (Signal for each word as the children say:) *He* (pause) *was* (pause) *mad.*
- (Repeat until firm.)

c. Everybody, write the sentence. Spell each word the right way. (As you check children's responses, remind the children:) Don't forget to put a period at the end of your sentence.

SPELLING LESSON 86

WORD WRITING
EXERCISE 1

Children write **if, am**

a. You're going to write the word **if.** Think about the sounds in (pause) **if** and write the word. ✔

To Correct

1. Say the sounds in **if.** (Signal.) *iiifff.*
2. Say the sounds the hard way. (Signal.) *iii* (pause) *fff.*
3. Write the word **if.** ✔

b. (Repeat step *a* for **am.**)

EXERCISE 2

Children write **arm, farm**

a. You're going to write the word (pause) **arm.** When you write the word (pause) **arm,** you write these sounds. **Aaa** (pause) **rrr** (pause) **mmm.**
b. Say the sounds you write for (pause) **arm.** (Signal for each sound as the children say:) *aaa* (pause) *rrr* (pause) *mmm.* (The children are to pause two seconds between sounds.)
- (Repeat until firm.)
c. Everybody, write the word (pause) **arm.** ✔
d. Now you're going to write the word (pause) **farm.** When you write the word (pause) **farm,** you write these sounds. **Fff** (pause) **aaa** (pause) **rrr** (pause) **mmm.**
e. Say the sounds you write for (pause) **farm.** (Signal for each sound as the children say:) *fff* (pause) *aaa* (pause) *rrr* (pause) *mmm.* (The children are to pause two seconds between sounds.)

- (Repeat until firm.)
  f. Everybody, write the word (pause) **farm.** ✔

EXERCISE 3

Children write **can**

a. You're going to write the word (pause) **can.** This word is tough. I'll say the sounds in (pause) **can** the hard way. Listen. **K** (pause) **aaa** (pause) **nnn.**

b. Your turn. Say the sounds in (pause) **can.** Get ready. (Signal for each sound as the children say:) *k* (pause) *aaa* (pause) *nnn.* (The children are to pause two seconds between the sounds.)

- (Repeat until firm.)

c. Everybody, write the word (pause) **can.** ✔

EXERCISE 4

Children write **did**

You're going to write the word **did.** Think about the sounds in (pause) **did** and write the word. ✔

> **To Correct** ————————
> 1. Say the sounds in **did.** (Signal.) *diiid.*
> 2. Say the sounds the hard way. (Signal.) *d* (pause) *iii* (pause) *d.*
> 3. Write the word **did.** ✔

SENTENCE WRITING
EXERCISE 5

Children write a sentence

a. Listen to this sentence. **He was fat.** Say the sentence. Get ready. (Signal.) *He was fat.*

b. Now you're going to say it the slow way. Get ready. (Signal for each word as the children say:) *He* (pause) *was* (pause) *fat.*

- (Repeat until firm.)

c. Everybody, write the sentence. Spell each word the right way. (As you check children's responses, remind the children:) Don't forget to put a period at the end of your sentence.

SPELLING LESSON 87

WORD WRITING
EXERCISE 1

Children write **ant, sun, can**

a. You're going to write the word **ant.** Think about the sounds in (pause) **ant** and write the word. ✔

> **To Correct** ————————
> 1. Say the sounds in **ant.** (Signal.) *aaannnt.*
> 2. Say the sounds the hard way. (Signal.) *aaa* (pause) *nnn* (pause) *t.*
> 3. Write the word **ant.** ✔

b. (Repeat step *a* for **sun** and **can.**)

EXERCISE 2

Children write **arm, farm**

a. You're going to write the word (pause) **arm.** When you write the word (pause) **arm,** you write these sounds. **Aaa** (pause) **rrr** (pause) **mmm.**

b. Say the sounds you write for (pause) **arm.** (Signal for each sound as the children say:) *aaa* (pause) *rrr* (pause) *mmm.* (The children are to pause two seconds between sounds.)

- (Repeat until firm.)

c. Everybody, write the word (pause) **arm.** ✔

d. Now you're going to write the word (pause) **farm.** When you write the word (pause) **farm,** you write these sounds. **Fff** (pause) **aaa** (pause) **rrr** (pause) **mmm.**

e. Say the sounds you write for (pause) **farm.** (Signal for each sound as the children say:) *fff* (pause) *aaa* (pause) *rrr* (pause) *mmm.* (The children are to pause two seconds between sounds.)

- (Repeat until firm.)

f. Everybody, write the word (pause) **farm.** ✔

EXERCISE 3

Children write **hot**

You're going to write the word **hot.** Think about the sounds in (pause) **hot** and write the word. ✔

SENTENCE WRITING
EXERCISE 4

Children write a sentence

a. Listen to this sentence. **It is a nut.** Your turn. Say the sentence. Get ready. (Signal.) *It is a nut.*

b. Now you're going to say it the slow way. Get ready. (Signal for each word as the children say:) *It* (pause) *is* (pause) *a* (pause) *nut.*

• (Repeat until firm.)

c. Everybody, write the sentence. Spell each word the right way. (As you check children's responses, remind the children:) Don't forget to put a period at the end of your sentence.

SPELLING LESSON 88

WORD WRITING
EXERCISE 1

Children write **arm**

a. You're going to write the word (pause) **arm.** Say the sounds you write for (pause) **arm.** Get ready. (Signal for each sound as the children say:) *aaa* (pause) *rrr* (pause) *mmm.* (The children are to pause two seconds between the sounds.)

• (Repeat until firm.)

b. Everybody, write the word (pause) **arm.** ✔

EXERCISE 2

Children write **not, and**

a. You're going to write the word **not.** Think about the sounds in (pause) **not** and write the word. ✔

To Correct

1. Say the sounds in **not.** (Signal.) *nnnooot.*
2. Say the sounds the hard way. (Signal.) *nnn* (pause) *ooo* (pause) *t.*
3. Write the word **not.** ✔

---

b. (Repeat step *a* for **and.**)

EXERCISE 3

Children write **farm**

a. You're going to write the word (pause) **farm.** Say the sounds you write for (pause) **farm.** Get ready. (Signal for each sound as the children say:) *fff* (pause) *aaa* (pause) *rrr* (pause) *mmm.* (The children are to pause two seconds between the sounds.)

• (Repeat until firm.)

b. Everybody, write the word (pause) **farm.** ✔

EXERCISE 4

Children write **hid**

You're going to write the word **hid.** Think about the sounds in (pause) **hid** and write the word. ✔

SENTENCE WRITING
EXERCISE 5

Children write a sentence

a. Listen to this sentence. **It is hot.** Your turn. Say the sentence. Get ready. (Signal.) *It is hot.*

b. Now you're going to say it the slow way. Get ready. (Signal for each word as the children say:) *It* (pause) *is* (pause) *hot.*

• (Repeat until firm.)

c. Everybody, write the sentence. Spell each word the right way. ✔

SPELLING LESSON 89

WORD WRITING
EXERCISE 1

Children write **farm**

a. You're going to write the word (pause) **farm.** Say the sounds you write for (pause) **farm.** Get ready. (Signal for each sound as the children say:) *fff* (pause) *aaa* (pause) *rrr* (pause) *mmm.* (The children are to pause two seconds between the sounds.)
• (Repeat until firm.)
b. Everybody, write the word (pause) **farm.** ✔

EXERCISE 2

Children write **can**

You're going to write the word **can.** Think about the sounds in (pause) **can** and write the word. ✔

> **To Correct**
> 1. Say the sounds in **can.** (Signal.) *kaaannn.*
> 2. Say the sounds the hard way. (Signal.) *k* (pause) *aaa* (pause) *nnn.*
> 3. Write the word **can.** ✔

EXERCISE 3

Children write **car**

a. You're going to write the word (pause) **car.** When you write the word (pause) **car,** you write these sounds. **K** (pause) **aaa** (pause) **rrr.**
b. Say the sounds you write for (pause) **car.** (Signal for each sound as the children say:) *k* (pause) *aaa* (pause) *rrr.* (The children are to pause two seconds between sounds.)
• (Repeat until firm.)
c. Everybody, write the word (pause) **car.** ✔

EXERCISE 4

Children write **me, sand, hid**

a. You're going to write the word **me.** Think about the sounds in (pause) **me** and write the word. ✔
b. (Repeat step *a* for **sand** and **hid.**)

SENTENCE WRITING
EXERCISE 5

Children write a sentence

a. Listen to this sentence. **He had a fan.** Your turn. Say the sentence. Get ready. (Signal.) *He had a fan.*
b. Now you're going to say it the slow way. Get ready. (Signal for each word as the children say:) *He* (pause) *had* (pause) *a* (pause) *fan.*
• (Repeat until firm.)
c. Everybody, write the sentence. Spell each word the right way. ✔

SPELLING LESSON 90

WORD WRITING
EXERCISE 1

Children write **and, mud, hot**

a. You're going to write the word **and.** Think about the sounds in (pause) **and** and write the word. ✔

> **To Correct**
> 1. Say the sounds in **and.** (Signal.) *aaannnd.*
> 2. Say the sounds the hard way. (Signal.) *aaa* (pause) *nnn* (pause) *d.*
> 3. Write the word **and.** ✔

b. (Repeat step *a* for **mud** and **hot.**)

EXERCISE 2

Children write **arm**

a. You're going to write the word (pause) **arm.** Say the sounds you write for (pause) **arm.** Get ready. (Signal for each sound as the children say:) *aaa* (pause) *rrr* (pause) *mmm.* (The children are to pause two seconds between the sounds.)

- (Repeat until firm.)
b. Everybody, write the word (pause) **arm.** ✔

EXERCISE 3

Children write **car**

a. You're going to write the word (pause) **car.** When you write the word (pause) **car,** you write these sounds. **K** (pause) **aaa** (pause) **rrr.**

b. Say the sounds you write for (pause) **car.** (Signal for each sound as the children say:) *k* (pause) *aaa* (pause) *rrr.* (The children are to pause two seconds between sounds.)

- (Repeat until firm.)
c. Everybody, write the word (pause) **car.** ✔

EXERCISE 4

Children write **can**

You're going to write the word **can.** Think about the sounds in (pause) **can** and write the word. ✔

SENTENCE WRITING
EXERCISE 5

Children write a sentence

a. Listen to this sentence. **His dad is sad.** Your turn. Say the sentence. Get ready. (Signal.) *His dad is sad.*

b. Now you're going to say it the slow way. Get ready. (Signal for each word as the children say:) *His* (pause) *dad* (pause) *is* (pause) *sad.*

- (Repeat until firm.)
c. Everybody, write the sentence. Spell each word the right way. ✔

SPELLING LESSON 91

WORD WRITING
EXERCISE 1

Children write **car, far, tar**

a. You're going to write the word (pause) **car.** When you write the word (pause) **car,** you write these sounds. **K** (pause) **aaa** (pause) **rrr.**

b. Say the sounds you write for (pause) **car.** (Signal for each sound as the children say:) *k* (pause) *aaa* (pause) *rrr.* (The children are to pause two seconds between sounds.)

- (Repeat until firm.)
c. Everybody, write the word (pause) **car.** ✔

d. Now you're going to write the word (pause) **far.** When you write the word (pause) **far,** you write these sounds. **Fff** (pause) **aaa** (pause) **rrr.**

e. Say the sounds you write for (pause) **far.** (Signal for each sound as the children say:) *fff* (pause) *aaa* (pause) *rrr.* (The children are to pause two seconds between sounds.)

- (Repeat until firm.)
f. Everybody, write the word (pause) **far.** ✔

g. Next you're going to write the word (pause) **tar.** When you write the word (pause) **tar,** you write these sounds. **T** (pause) **aaa** (pause) **rrr.**

h. Say the sounds you write for (pause) **tar.** (Signal for each sound as the children say:) *t* (pause) *aaa* (pause) *rrr.* (The children are to pause two seconds between sounds.)

- (Repeat until firm.)
i. Everybody, write the word (pause) **tar.** ✔

EXERCISE 2

Children write **arm, farm**

a. You're going to write the word **arm.** Think about the sounds in (pause) **arm** and write the word. ✔

To Correct

1. Say the sounds the hard way. (Signal.) *aaa* (pause) *rrr* (pause) *mmm.*
2. Write the word **arm.** ✔

b. (Repeat step *a* for **farm.**)

SENTENCE WRITING
EXERCISE 3

Children write a sentence

a. Listen to this sentence. **His dad has sand.** Your turn. Say that sentence. Get ready. (Signal.) *His dad has sand.*

b. Now you're going to say it the slow way. Get ready. (Signal for each word as the children say:) *His* (pause) *dad* (pause) *has* (pause) *sand.*

• (Repeat until firm.)

c. Everybody, write the sentence. Spell each word the right way. ✔

SPELLING LESSON 92

WORD WRITING
EXERCISE 1

Children write **are**

a. You're going to write the word (pause) **are.** When you write the word (pause) **are,** you write these sounds. **Aaa** (pause) **rrr** (pause) **ēēē.**

b. Say the sounds you write for (pause) **are.** (Signal for each sound as the children say:) *aaa* (pause) *rrr* (pause) *ēēē.* (The children are to pause two seconds between sounds.)

• (Repeat until firm.)

c. Everybody, write the word (pause) **are.** ✔

EXERCISE 2

Children write **far, car**

a. You're going to write the word (pause) **far.** Say the sounds you write for (pause) **far.** Get ready. (Signal for each sound as the children say:) *fff* (pause) *aaa* (pause) *rrr.* (The children are to pause two seconds between the sounds.)

• (Repeat until firm.)

b. Everybody, write the word (pause) **far.** ✔

c. Now you're going to write the word (pause) **car.**

• Say the sounds you write for (pause) **car.** (Signal for each sound as the children say:) *k* (pause) *aaa* (pause) *rrr.* (The children are to pause two seconds between sounds.)

• (Repeat until firm.)

d. Everybody, write the word (pause) **car.** ✔

EXERCISE 3

Children write **not, land**

a. You're going to write the word **not.** Think about the sounds in (pause) **not,** and write the word. ✔

To Correct

1. Say the sounds in **not.** (Signal.) *nnnooot.*
2. Say the sounds the hard way. (Signal.) *nnn* (pause) *ooo* (pause) *t.*
3. Write the word **not.** ✔

b. (Repeat step *a* for **land.**)

SENTENCE WRITING
EXERCISE 4

Children write a sentence

a. Listen to this sentence. **He has a dad.** Your turn. Say that sentence. Get ready. (Signal.) *He has a dad.*

b. Now you're going to say it the slow way. Get ready. (Signal for each word as the children say:) *He* (pause) *has* (pause) *a* (pause) *dad.*

• (Repeat until firm.)

c. Everybody, write the sentence. Spell each word the right way. ✔

Spelling Lesson 93

WORD WRITING
EXERCISE 1

Children write **car**

a. You're going to write the word (pause) **car.** Say the sounds you write for (pause) **car.** Get ready. (Signal for each sound as the children say:) *k* (pause) *aaa* (pause) *rrr.* (The children are to pause two seconds between the sounds.)
• (Repeat until firm.)
b. Everybody, write the word (pause) **car.** ✔

EXERCISE 2

Children write **tan**

You're going to write the word **tan.** Think about the sounds in (pause) **tan** and write the word. ✔

> **To Correct**
> 1. Say the sounds in **tan.** (Signal.) *taaannn.*
> 2. Say the sounds the hard way. (Signal.) *t* (pause) *aaa* (pause) *nnn.*
> 3. Write the word **tan.** ✔

EXERCISE 3

Children write **are**

a. You're going to write the word (pause) **are.** When you write the word (pause) **are,** you write these sounds. **Aaa** (pause) **rrr** (pause) **ēēē.**
b. Say the sounds you write for (pause) **are.** (Signal for each sound as the children say:) *aaa* (pause) *rrr* (pause) *ēēē.* (The children are to pause two seconds between sounds.)
• (Repeat until firm.)
c. Write the word (pause) **are.** ✔

EXERCISE 4

Children write **was, can**

a. You're going to write the word **was.** Think about the sounds in (pause) **was** and write the word. ✔

> **To Correct**
> 1. Say the sounds the hard way. (Signal.) *www* (pause) *aaa* (pause) *sss.*
> 2. Write the word **was.** ✔

b. (Repeat step *a* for **can.**)

EXERCISE 5

Children write **far**

a. You're going to write the word (pause) **far.** Say the sounds you write for (pause) **far.** Get ready. (Signal for each sound as the children say:) *fff* (pause) *aaa* (pause) *rrr.* (The children are to pause two seconds between the sounds.)
• (Repeat until firm.)
b. Everybody, write the word (pause) **far.** ✔

SENTENCE WRITING
EXERCISE 6

Children write a sentence

a. Listen to this sentence. **A farm is fun.** Your turn. Say that sentence. Get ready. (Signal.) *A farm is fun.*
b. Now you're going to say it the slow way. Get ready. (Signal for each word as the children say:) *A* (pause) *farm* (pause) *is* (pause) *fun.*
• (Repeat until firm.)
c. Everybody, write the sentence. Spell each word the right way. ✔

Spelling Lesson 94

WORD WRITING
EXERCISE 1

Children write **are**

a. You're going to write the word (pause) **are.** Say the sounds you write for (pause) **are.** Get ready. (Signal for each sound as the children say:) *aaa* (pause) *rrr* (pause) *ēēē.* (The children are to pause two seconds between the sounds.)
• (Repeat until firm.)

b. Everybody, write the word (pause) **are.** ✔

EXERCISE 2

Children write **hard**

a. You're going to write the word (pause) **hard.** When you write the word (pause) **hard,** you write these sounds. **H** (pause) **aaa** (pause) **rrr** (pause) **d.**

b. Say the sounds you write for (pause) **hard.** (Signal for each sound as the children say:) *h* (pause) *aaa* (pause) *rrr* (pause) *d.* (The children are to pause two seconds between sounds.)

• (Repeat until firm.)

c. Everybody, write the word (pause) **hard.** ✔

EXERCISE 3

Children write **car**

a. You're going to write the word (pause) **car.** Say the sounds you write for (pause) **car.** Get ready. (Signal for each sound as the children say:) *k* (pause) *aaa* (pause) *rrr.* (The children are to pause two seconds between the sounds.)

• (Repeat until firm.)

b. Everybody, write the word (pause) **car.** ✔

EXERCISE 4

Children write **card**

a. You're going to write the word (pause) **card.** When you write the word (pause) **card,** you write these sounds. **K** (pause) **aaa** (pause) **rrr** (pause) **d.**

b. Say the sounds you write for (pause) **card.** (Signal for each sound as the children say:) *k* (pause) *aaa* (pause) *rrr* (pause) *d.* (The children are to pause two seconds between the sounds.)

• (Repeat until firm.)

c. Everybody, write the word (pause) **card.** ✔

EXERCISE 5

Children write **nod**

You're going to write the word **nod.** Think about the sounds in (pause) **nod** and write the word. ✔

To Correct

1. Say the sounds in **nod.** (Signal.) *nnnoood.*
2. Say the sounds the hard way. (Signal.) *nnn* (pause) *ooo* (pause) *d.*
3. Write the word **nod.** ✔

SENTENCE WRITING
EXERCISE 6

Children write a sentence

a. Listen to this sentence. **I am not sad.** Your turn. Say that sentence. Get ready. (Signal.) *I am not sad.*

b. Now you're going to say it the slow way. Get ready. (Signal for each word as the children say:) *I* (pause) *am* (pause) *not* (pause) *sad.*

• (Repeat until firm.)

c. Everybody, write the sentence. Spell each word the right way. ✔

SPELLING LESSON 95

SOUND WRITING
EXERCISE 1

Children write **b**

a. You're going to write a sound.

b. Here's the sound you're going to write. Listen. **b.** What sound? (Signal.) *b.*

c. Write **b.** ✔

WORD WRITING
EXERCISE 2

Children write **we, hid**

a. You're going to write the word **we.** Think about the sounds in (pause) **we** and write the word. ✔

To Correct

1. Say the sounds in **we.** (Signal.) *wwwēēē.*
2. Say the sounds the hard way. (Signal.) *www* (pause) *ēēē.*
3. Write the word **we.** ✔

b. (Repeat step *a* for **hid.**)

EXERCISE 3

Children write **are**

a. You're going to write the word (pause) **are.** Say the sounds you write for (pause) **are.** Get ready. (Signal for each sound as the children say:) *aaa* (pause) *rrr* (pause) *ēēē.* (The children are to pause two seconds between the sounds.)

• (Repeat until firm.)

b. Everybody, write the word (pause) **are.** ✔

EXERCISE 4

Children write **was, has, can**

a. You're going to write the word **was.** Think about the sounds in (pause) **was** and write the word. ✔

> **To Correct**
> 1. Say the sounds the hard way. (Signal.) *www* (pause) *aaa* (pause) *sss.*
> 2. Write the word **was.** ✔

b. (Repeat step *a* for **has** and **can.**)

SENTENCE WRITING
EXERCISE 5

Children write a sentence

a. Listen to this sentence. **His dad was mad.** Your turn. Say that sentence. Get ready. (Signal.) *His dad was mad.*

b. Now you're going to say it the slow way. Get ready. (Signal for each word as the children say:) *His* (pause) *dad* (pause) *was* (pause) *mad.*

• (Repeat until firm.)

c. Everybody, write the sentence. Spell each word the right way. ✔

SPELLING LESSON 96

SOUND WRITING
EXERCISE 1

Children write **b**

a. You're going to write a sound.

b. Here's the sound you're going to write. Listen. **b.** What sound? (Signal.) *b.*

c. Write **b.** ✔

WORD WRITING
EXERCISE 2

Children write **are, sit**

a. You're going to write the word **are.** Think about the sounds in (pause) **are** and write the word. ✔

> **To Correct**
> 1. Say the sounds the hard way. (Signal.) *aaa* (pause) *rrr* (pause) *ēēē.*
> 2. Write the word **are.** ✔

b. (Repeat step *a* for **sit.**)

EXERCISE 3

Children write **bit**

a. You're going to write the word (pause) **bit.** This word is tough. I'll say the sounds in (pause) **bit** the hard way. Listen. **B** (pause) **iii** (pause) **t.**

b. Your turn. Say the sounds in (pause) **bit.** Get ready. (Signal for each sound as the children say:) *b* (pause) *iii* (pause) *t.* (The children are to pause two seconds between sounds.)

• (Repeat until firm.)

c. Everybody, write the word (pause) **bit.** ✔

EXERCISE 4

Children write **land**

You're going to write the word **land.** Think about the sounds in (pause) **land** and write the word. ✔

EXERCISE 5

Children write **card**

a. You're going to write the word (pause) **card.** Say the sounds you write for (pause) **card.** Get ready. (Signal for each sound as the children say:) *k* (pause) *aaa* (pause) *rrr* (pause) *d.* (The children are to pause two seconds between the sounds.)

- (Repeat until firm.)
b. Everybody, write the word (pause) **card.** ✔

EXERCISE 6

Children write **cat**

a. You're going to write the word **cat.** Listen. **Cat.** Saying the sounds in (pause) **cat** the hard way. Get ready. (Signal for each sound as the children say:) *k* (pause) *aaa* (pause) *t.* (The children are to pause two seconds between the sounds.)
- (Repeat until firm.)
b. Everybody, write the word (pause) **cat.** ✔

SENTENCE WRITING
EXERCISE 7

Children write a sentence

a. Listen to this sentence. **I am not fat.** Your turn. Say that sentence. Get ready. (Signal.) *I am not fat.*
b. Now you're going to say it the slow way. Get ready. (Signal for each word as the children say:) *I* (pause) *am* (pause) *not* (pause) *fat.*
- (Repeat until firm.)
c. Everybody, write the sentence. Spell each word the right way. ✔

SPELLING LESSON 97

WORD WRITING
EXERCISE 1

Children write **card, farm, is**

a. You're going to write the word **card.** Think about the sounds in (pause) **card** and write the word. ✔

> **To Correct**
> 1. Say the sounds the hard way. (Signal.) *k* (pause) *aaa* (pause) *rrr* (pause) *d.*
> 2. Write the word **card.** ✔

b. (Repeat step *a* for **farm** and **is.**)

EXERCISE 2

Children write **bit**

a. You're going to write the word (pause) **bit.** This word is tough. I'll say the sounds in (pause) **bit** the hard way. Listen. **B** (pause) **iii** (pause) **t.**
b. Your turn. Say the sounds in (pause) **bit.** Get ready. (Signal for each sound as the children say:) *b* (pause) *iii* (pause) *t.* (The children are to pause two seconds between the sounds.)
- (Repeat until firm.)
c. Everybody, write the word (pause) **bit.** ✔

EXERCISE 3

Children write **not**

You're going to write the word **not.** Think about the sounds in (pause) **not** and write the word.

> **To Correct**
> 1. Say the sounds in **not.** (Signal.) *nnnooot.*
> 2. Say the sounds the hard way. (Signal.) *nnn* (pause) *ooo* (pause) *t.*
> 3. Write the word **not.** ✔

SENTENCE WRITING
EXERCISE 4

Children write a sentence

a. Listen to this sentence. **He did run far.** Your turn. Say that sentence. Get ready. (Signal.) *He did run far.*
b. Now you're going to say it the slow way. Get ready. (Signal for each word as the children say:) *He* (pause) *did* (pause) *run* (pause) *far.*
- (Repeat until firm.)
c. Everybody, write the sentence. Spell each word the right way. ✔

Spelling Lesson 98

WORD WRITING
EXERCISE 1

Children write **bad**

a. You're going to write the word (pause) **bad.** This word is tough. I'll say the sounds in (pause) **bad** the hard way. Listen. **B** (pause) **aaa** (pause) **d.**

b. Your turn. Say the sounds in (pause) **bad.** Get ready. (Signal for each sound as the children say:) *b* (pause) *aaa* (pause) *d.* (The children are to pause two seconds between the sounds.)

• (Repeat until firm.)

c. Everybody, write the word (pause) **bad.** ✔

EXERCISE 2

Children write **are, his, card**

a. You're going to write the word **are.** Think about the sounds in (pause) **are** and write the word. ✔

> **To Correct**
> 1. Say the sounds the hard way. (Signal.) *aaa* (pause) *rrr* (pause) *ēēē.*
> 2. Write the word **are.** ✔

b. (Repeat step *a* for **his** and **card.**)

EXERCISE 3

Children write **cart**

a. You're going to write the word (pause) **cart.** Say the sounds you write for (pause) **cart.** Get ready. (Signal for each sound as the children say:) *k* (pause) *aaa* (pause) *rrr* (pause) *t.* (The children are to pause two seconds between the sounds.)

• (Repeat until firm.)

b. Everybody, write the word (pause) **cart.** ✔

EXERCISE 4

Children write **cat**

a. You're going to write the word **cat.** Listen. **Cat.** Saying the sounds in (pause) **cat** the hard way. Get ready. (Signal for each sound as the children say:) *k* (pause) *aaa* (pause) *t.* (The children are to pause two seconds between the sounds.)

• (Repeat until firm.)

b. Everybody, write the word (pause) **cat.** ✔

SENTENCE WRITING
EXERCISE 5

Children write a sentence

a. Listen to this sentence. **We are not sad.** Your turn. Say that sentence. Get ready. (Signal.) *We are not sad.*

b. Now you're going to say it the slow way. Get ready. (Signal for each word as the children say:) *We* (pause) *are* (pause) *not* (pause) *sad.*

• (Repeat until firm.)

c. Everybody, write the sentence. Spell each word the right way. ✔

Spelling Lesson 99

WORD WRITING
EXERCISE 1

Children write **was, can**

a. You're going to write the word **was.** Think about the sounds in (pause) **was** and write the word. ✔

> **To Correct**
> 1. Say the sounds the hard way. (Signal.) *www* (pause) *aaa* (pause) *sss.*
> 2. Write the word **was.** ✔

b. You're going to write the word **can.** Think about the sounds in (pause) **can** and write the word. ✔

> **To Correct**
>
> 1. Say the sounds in **can.** (Signal.)
>   *kaaannn.*
> 2. Say the sounds the hard way. (Signal.)
>   *k* (pause) *aaa* (pause) *nnn.*

EXERCISE 2

Children write **cat**

a. You're going to write the word **cat.** Listen. **Cat.** Saying the sounds in (pause) **cat** the hard way. Get ready. (Signal for each sound as the children say:) *k* (pause) *aaa* (pause) *t.* (The children are to pause two seconds between the sounds.)
• (Repeat until firm.)
b. Everybody, write the word (pause) **cat.** ✔

EXERCISE 3

Children write **see**

a. You're going to write the word (pause) **see.** When you write the word (pause) **see,** you write these sounds. **Sss** (pause) *ēēē* (pause) *ēēē.*
b. Say the sounds you write for (pause) **see.** (Signal for each sound as the children say:) *sss* (pause) *ēēē* (pause) *ēēē.* (The children are to pause two seconds between sounds.)
• (Repeat until firm.)
c. Write the word (pause) **see.** ✔

EXERCISE 4

Children write **farm**

You're going to write the word **farm.** Think about the sounds in (pause) **farm** and write the word. ✔

EXERCISE 5

Children write **but**

a. You're going to write the word (pause) **but.** This word is tough. I'll say the sounds in (pause) **but** the hard way. Listen. **B** (pause) **uuu** (pause) **t.**

b. Your turn. Say the sounds in (pause) **but.** Get ready. (Signal for each sound as the children say:) *b* (pause) *uuu* (pause) *t.* (The children are to pause two seconds between sounds.)
• (Repeat until firm.)
c. Everybody, write the word (pause) **but.** ✔

SENTENCE WRITING
EXERCISE 6

Children write a sentence

a. Listen to this sentence. **I am in mud.** Your turn. Say that sentence. Get ready. (Signal.) *I am in mud.*
b. Now you're going to say it the slow way. Get ready. (Signal for each word as the children say:) *I* (pause) *am* (pause) *in* (pause) *mud.*
• (Repeat until firm.)
c. Everybody, write the sentence. Spell each word the right way. ✔

SPELLING LESSON 100

WORD WRITING
EXERCISE 1

Children write **see**

a. You're going to write the word (pause) **see.** When you write the word (pause) **see,** you write these sounds. **Sss** (pause) *ēēē* (pause) *ēēē.*
b. Say the sounds you write for (pause) **see.** (Signal for each sound as the children say:) *sss* (pause) *ēēē* (pause) *ēēē.* (The children are to pause two seconds between sounds.)
• (Repeat until firm.)
c. Write the word (pause) **see.** ✔

EXERCISE 2

Children write **but**

a. You're going to write the word (pause) **but.** This word is tough. I'll say the sounds in (pause) **but** the hard way. Listen. **B** (pause) **uuu** (pause) **t.**

b. Your turn. Say the sounds in (pause) **but.** Get ready. (Signal for each sound as the children say:) *b* (pause) *uuu* (pause) *t.* (The children are to pause two seconds between the sounds.)
- (Repeat until firm.)

c. Everybody, write the word (pause) **but.** ✔

EXERCISE 3

Children write **his**

You're going to write the word **his.** Think about the sounds in (pause) **his** and write the word. ✔

> **To Correct**
> 1. Say the sounds the hard way. (Signal.) *h* (pause) *iii* (pause) *sss.*
> 2. Write the word **his.** ✔

EXERCISE 4

Children write **bit**

a. You're going to write the word **bit.** Listen. **Bit.** Saying the sounds in (pause) **bit** the hard way. Get ready. (Signal for each sound as the children say:) *b* (pause) *iii* (pause) *t.* (The children are to pause two seconds between the sounds.)
- (Repeat until firm.)

b. Everybody, write the word (pause) **bit.** ✔

SENTENCE WRITING
EXERCISE 5

Children write a sentence

a. Listen to this sentence. **We are in sand.** Your turn. Say the sentence. Get ready. (Signal.) *We are in sand.*

b. Now you're going to say it the slow way. Get ready. (Signal for each word as the children say:) *We* (pause) *are* (pause) *in* (pause) *sand.*
- (Repeat until firm.)

c. Everybody, write the sentence. Spell each word the right way. ✔

SPELLING LESSON 101

WORD WRITING
EXERCISE 1

Children write **bad**

a. You're going to write the word (pause) **bad.** Say the sounds you write for (pause) **bad.** Get ready. (Signal for each sound as the children say:) *b* (pause) *aaa* (pause) *d.* (The children are to pause two seconds between the sounds.)
- (Repeat until firm.)

b. Everybody, write the word (pause) **bad.** ✔

EXERCISE 2

Children write **see**

a. You're going to write the word (pause) **see.** When you write the word (pause) **see,** you write these sounds. **Sss** (pause) *ēēē* (pause) *ēēē.*

b. Say the sounds you write for (pause) **see.** (Signal for each sound as the children say:) *sss* (pause) *ēēē* (pause) *ē ēē.* (The children are to pause two seconds between sounds.)
- (Repeat until firm.)

c. Write the word (pause) **see.** ✔

EXERCISE 3

Children write **but**

a. You're going to write the word (pause) **but.** Say the sounds you write for (pause) **but.** Get ready. (Signal for each sound as the children say:) *b* (pause) *uuu* (pause) *t.* (The children are to pause two seconds between the sounds.)
- (Repeat until firm.)

b. Everybody, write the word (pause) **but.** ✔

EXERCISE 4

Children write **and**

You're going to write the word **and.** Think about the sounds in (pause) **and** and write the word. ✔

EXERCISE 5

Children write **bit**

a. You're going to write the word (pause) **bit.** Say the sounds you write for (pause) **bit.** Get ready. (Signal for each sound as the children say:) *b* (pause) *iii* (pause) *t.* (The children are to pause two seconds between the sounds.)
- (Repeat until firm.)
b. Everybody, write the word (pause) **bit.** ✔

SENTENCE WRITING
EXERCISE 6

Children write a sentence

a. Listen to this sentence. **We are on land.** Your turn. Say that sentence. Get ready. (Signal.) *We are on land.*
b. Now you're going to say it the slow way. Get ready. (Signal for each word as the children say:) *We* (pause) *are* (pause) *on* (pause) *land.*
- (Repeat until firm.)
c. Everybody, write the sentence. Spell each word the right way. ✔

SPELLING LESSON 102

SOUND WRITING
EXERCISE 1

Children write **th**

a. You're going to write a sound.
b. Here's the sound you're going to write. Listen. **ththth.** What sound? (Signal.) *ththth.*
c. Write **ththth.** ✔

WORD WRITING
EXERCISE 2

Children write **bit**

You're going to write the word **bit.** Think about the sounds in (pause) **bit** and write the word. ✔

To Correct

1. Say the sounds in **bit.** (Signal.) *biiit.*
2. Say the sounds the hard way. (Signal.) *b* (pause) *iii* (pause) *t.*
3. Write the word **bit.** ✔

EXERCISE 3

Children write **see**

a. You're going to write the word (pause) **see.** Say the sounds you write for (pause) **see.** Get ready. (Signal for each sound as the children say:) *sss* (pause) *ēēē* (pause) *ēēē.* (The children are to pause two seconds between the sounds.)
- (Repeat until firm.)
b. Everybody, write the word (pause) **see.** ✔

EXERCISE 4

Children write **can, but, card**

a. You're going to write the word **can.** Think about the sounds in (pause) **can** and write the word. ✔
b. (Repeat step *a* for **but.**)
c. You're going to write the word **card.** Think about the sounds in (pause) **card** and write the word.

To Correct

1. Say the sounds the hard way. (Signal.) *k* (pause) *aaa* (pause) *rrr* (pause) *d.*
2. Write the word **card.** ✔

SENTENCE WRITING
EXERCISE 5

Children write a sentence

a. Listen to this sentence. **We had a car.** Your turn. Say that sentence. Get ready. (Signal.) *We had a car.*
b. Now you're going to say it the slow way. Get ready. (Signal for each word as the children say:) *We* (pause) *had* (pause) *a* (pause) *car.*
- (Repeat until firm.)

c. Everybody, write the sentence. Spell each word the right way. ✔

SPELLING LESSON 103

SOUND WRITING
EXERCISE 1

Children write **th**

a. You're going to write a sound.
b. Here's the sound you're going to write. Listen. **ththth.** What sound? (Signal.) *ththth.*
c. Write **ththth.** ✔

WORD WRITING
EXERCISE 2

Children write **are, bad**

a. You're going to write the word **are.** Think about the sounds in (pause) **are** and write the word. ✔

> **To Correct**
> 1. Say the sounds the hard way. (Signal.) *aaa* (pause) *rrr* (pause) *ēēē.*
> 2. Write the word **are.** ✔

b. (Repeat step *a* for **bad.**)

EXERCISE 3

Children write **thē**

a. You're going to write the word (pause) **thē.** This word is tough. I'll say the sounds in (pause) **thē** the hard way. Listen. **Ththth** (pause) *ēēē.*
b. Your turn. Say the sounds in (pause) **thē.** Get ready. (Signal for each sound as the children say:) *ththth* (pause) *ēēē.* (The children are to pause two seconds between the sounds.)
• (Repeat until firm.)
c. Everybody, write the word (pause) **thē.** ✔

EXERCISE 4

Children write **this, that**

a. You're going to write the word **this.** Listen. **This.** Saying the sounds in (pause) **this** the hard way. Get ready. (Signal for each sound as the children say:) *ththth* (pause) *iii* (pause) *sss.* (The children are to pause two seconds between the sounds.)
• (Repeat until firm.)
b. Everybody, write the word (pause) **this.** ✔
c. (Repeat steps *a* and *b* for **that.**)

SENTENCE WRITING
EXERCISE 5

Children write a sentence

a. Listen to this sentence. **He has a farm.** Your turn. Say that sentence. Get ready. (Signal.) *He has a farm.*
b. Now you're going to say it the slow way. Get ready. (Signal for each word as the children say:) *He* (pause) *has* (pause) *a* (pause) *farm.*
• (Repeat until firm.)
c. Everybody, write the sentence. Spell each word the right way. ✔

SPELLING LESSON 104

WORD WRITING
EXERCISE 1

Children write **that**

a. You're going to write the word **that.** Listen. **That.** Saying the sounds in (pause) **that** the hard way. Get ready. (Signal for each sound as the children say:) *ththth* (pause) *aaa* (pause) *t.* (The children are to pause two seconds between the sounds.)
• (Repeat until firm.)
b. Everybody, write the word (pause) **that.** ✔

EXERCISE 2

Children write see

a. You're going to write the word (pause) **see.** Say the sounds you write for (pause) **see.** Get ready. (Signal for each sound as the children say:) *sss* (pause) *ēēē* (pause) *ēēē.* (The children are to pause two seconds between the sounds.)
- (Repeat until firm.)

b. Everybody, write the word (pause) **see.** ✔

EXERCISE 3

Children write thē

a. You're going to write the word **thē.** Listen. **Thē.** Saying the sounds in (pause) **thē** the hard way. Get ready. (Signal for each sound as the children say:) *ththth* (pause) *ēēē.* (The children are to pause two seconds between the sounds.)
- (Repeat until firm.)

b. Everybody, write the word (pause) **thē.** ✔

EXERCISE 4

Children write are

You're going to write the word **are.** Think about the sounds in (pause) **are** and write the word. ✔

> **To Correct**
> 1. Say the sounds the hard way. (Signal.) *aaa* (pause) *rrr* (pause) *ēēē.*
> 2. Write the word **are.** ✔

EXERCISE 5

Children write this

a. You're going to write the word **this.** Listen. **This.** Saying the sounds in (pause) **this** the hard way. Get ready. (Signal for each sound as the children say:) *ththth* (pause) *iii* (pause) *sss.* (The children are to pause two seconds between the sounds.)
- (Repeat until firm.)

b. Everybody, write the word (pause) **this.** ✔

SENTENCE WRITING
EXERCISE 6

Children write a sentence

a. Listen to this sentence. **He did not run.** Your turn. Say that sentence. Get ready. (Signal.) *He did not run.*

b. Now you're going to say it the slow way. Get ready. (Signal for each word as the children say:) *He* (pause) *did* (pause) *not* (pause) *run.*
- (Repeat until firm.)

c. Everybody, write the sentence. Spell each word the right way. ✔

SPELLING LESSON 105

WORD WRITING
EXERCISE 1

Children write will

a. You're going to write the word (pause) **will.** When you write the word (pause) **will,** you write these sounds. **Www** (pause) **iii** (pause) **lll** (pause) **lll.**

b. Say the sounds you write for (pause) **will.** (Signal for each sound as the children say:) *www* (pause) *iii* (pause) *lll* (pause) *lll.* (The children are to pause two seconds between sounds.)
- (Repeat until firm.)

c. Everybody, write the word (pause) **will.** ✔

EXERCISE 2

Children write arm

You're going to write the word **arm.** Think about the sounds in (pause) **arm** and write the word. ✔

> **To Correct**
> 1. Say the sounds the hard way. (Signal.) *aaa* (pause) *rrr* (pause) *mmm.*
> 2. Write the word **arm.** ✔

EXERCISE 3

Children write barn

a. You're going to write the word (pause) **barn.** When you write the word (pause) **barn,** you write these sounds. **B** (pause) **aaa** (pause) **rrr** (pause) **nnn.**

b. Say the sounds you write for (pause) **barn.** (Signal for each sound as the children say:) *b* (pause) *aaa* (pause) *rrr* (pause) *nnn.* (The children are to pause two seconds between sounds.)

• (Repeat until firm.)

c. Everybody, write the word (pause) **barn.** ✔

EXERCISE 4

Children write that

a. You're going to write the word **that.** Listen. **That.** Saying the sounds in (pause) **that** the hard way. Get ready. (Signal for each sound as the children say:) *ththth* (pause) *aaa* (pause) *t.* (The children are to pause two seconds between the sounds.)

• (Repeat until firm.)

b. Everybody, write the word (pause) **that.** ✔

EXERCISE 5

Children write can

You're going to write the word **can.** Think about the sounds in (pause) **can** and write the word. ✔

SENTENCE WRITING
EXERCISE 6

Children write a sentence

a. Listen to this sentence. **We are in the sand.** Your turn. Say that sentence. Get ready. (Signal.) *We are in the sand.*

b. Now you're going to say it the slow way. Get ready. (Signal for each word as the children say:) *We* (pause) *are* (pause) *in* (pause) *the* (pause) *sand.*

• (Repeat until firm.)

c. Everybody, write the sentence. Spell each word the right way. ✔

SPELLING LESSON 106

WORD WRITING
EXERCISE 1

Children write see

a. You're going to write the word (pause) **see.** Say the sounds you write for (pause) **see.** Get ready. (Signal for each sound as the children say:) *sss* (pause) *ēēē* (pause) *ēēē.* (The children are to pause two seconds between the sounds.)

• (Repeat until firm.)

b. Everybody, write the word (pause) **see.** ✔

EXERCISE 2

Children write this

You're going to write the word **this.** Think about the sounds in (pause) **this** and write the word. ✔

> ### To Correct
> 1. Say the sounds in **this.** (Signal.) *ththththiiisss.*
> 2. Say the sounds the hard way. (Signal.) *ththth* (pause) *iii* (pause) *sss.*
> 3. Write the word **this.** ✔

EXERCISE 3

Children write will

a. You're going to write the word (pause) **will.** When you write the word (pause) **will,** you write these sounds. **Www** (pause) **iii** (pause) **lll** (pause) **lll.**

b. Say the sounds you write for (pause) **will.** (Signal for each sound as the children say:) *www* (pause) *iii* (pause) *lll* (pause) *lll.* (The children are to pause two seconds between the sounds.)

• (Repeat until firm.)

c. Everybody, write the word (pause) **will.** ✔

EXERCISE 4

Children write barn

a. You're going to write the word (pause) **barn.** Say the sounds you write for (pause) **barn.** Get ready. (Signal for each sound as the children say:) *b* (pause) *aaa* (pause) *rrr* (pause) *nnn.* (The children are to pause two seconds between the sounds.)
• (Repeat until firm.)
b. Everybody, write the word (pause) **barn.** ✔

EXERCISE 5

Children write thē, cat

a. You're going to write the word **thē.** Think about the sounds in (pause) **the** and write the word. ✔

To Correct _____

1. Say the sounds in **thē.** (Signal.) *thththēēē.*
2. Say the sounds the hard way. (Signal.) *thathth* (pause) *ēēē.*
3. Write the word **thē.** ✔

b. (Repeat step *a* for **cat.**)

SENTENCE WRITING
EXERCISE 6

Children write a sentence

a. Listen to this sentence. **The ant was bad.** Your turn. Say that sentence. Get ready. (Signal.) *The ant was bad.*
b. Now you're going to say it the slow way. Get ready. (Signal for each word as the children say:) *The* (pause) *ant* (pause) *was* (pause) *bad.*
• (Repeat until firm.)
c. Everybody, write the sentence. Spell each word the right way. ✔

SPELLING LESSON 107

SOUND WRITING
EXERCISE 1

Children write p

a. You're going to write a sound.

b. Here's the sound you're going to write. Listen. **p.** What sound? (Signal.) *p.*
c. Write **p.** ✔

WORD WRITING
EXERCISE 2

Children write but, that, cat

a. You're going to write the word **but.** Think about the sounds in (pause) **but** and write the word. ✔

To Correct _____

1. Say the sounds in **but.** (Signal.) *buuut.*
2. Say the sounds the hard way. (Signal.) *b* (pause) *uuu* (pause) *t.*
3. Write the word **but.** ✔

b. (Repeat step *a* for **that** and **cat.**)

EXERCISE 3

Children write will

a. You're going to write the word (pause) **will.** Say the sounds you write for (pause) **will.** Get ready. (Signal for each sound as the children say:) *www* (pause) *iii* (pause) *lll* (pause) *lll.* (The children are to pause two seconds between the sounds.)
• (Repeat until firm.)
b. Everybody, write the word (pause) **will.** ✔

EXERCISE 4

Children write see

You're going to write the word **see.** Think about the sounds in (pause) **see** and write the word. ✔

To Correct _____

1. Say the sounds the hard way. (Signal.) *sss* (pause) *ēēē* (pause) *ēēē.*
2. Write the word **see.** ✔

66

SENTENCE WRITING
EXERCISE 5

Children write a sentence

a. Listen to this sentence. **This car is tan.** Your turn. Say that sentence. Get ready. (Signal.) *This car is tan.*

b. Now you're going to say it the slow way. Get ready. (Signal for each word as the children say:) *This* (pause) *car* (pause) *is* (pause) *tan.*

• (Repeat until firm.)

c. Everybody, write the sentence. Spell each word the right way. ✔

SPELLING LESSON 108

SOUND WRITING
EXERCISE 1

Children write **p**

a. You're going to write a sound.

b. Here's the sound you're going to write. Listen. **p.** What sound? (Signal.) *p.*

c. Write **p.** ✔

WORD WRITING
EXERCISE 2

Children write **bill**

a. You're going to write the word (pause) **bill.** When you write the word (pause) **bill,** you write these sounds.
B (pause) **iii** (pause) **lll** (pause) **lll.**

b. Say the sounds you write for (pause) **bill.** (Signal for each sound as the children say:) *b* (pause) *iii* (pause) *lll* (pause) *lll.* (The children are to pause two seconds between the sounds.)

• (Repeat until firm.)

c. Everybody, write the word (pause) **bill.** ✔

EXERCISE 3

Children write **will**

a. You're going to write the word (pause) **will.** Say the sounds you write for (pause) **will.** Get ready. (Signal for each sound as the children say:) *www* (pause) *iii* (pause) *lll* (pause) *lll.* (The children are to pause two seconds between the sounds.)

• (Repeat until firm.)

b. Everybody, write the word (pause) **will.** ✔

EXERCISE 4

Children write **are, the, but**

a. You're going to write the word **are.** Think about the sounds in (pause) **are** and write the word. ✔

> **To Correct**
> 1. Say the sounds the hard way. (Signal.) *aaa* (pause) *rrr* (pause) *ēēē.*
> 2. Write the word **are.** ✔

b. You're going to write the word **thē.** Think about the sounds in (pause) **thē** and write the word. ✔

> **To Correct**
> 1. Say the sounds in **thē.** (Signal.) *ththth ē ē ē.*
> 2. Say the sounds the hard way. (Signal.) *ththth* (pause) *ēēē.*
> 3. Write the word **thē.** ✔

c. (Repeat step *b* for **but.**)

SENTENCE WRITING
EXERCISE 5

Children write a sentence

a. Listen to this sentence. **It is a fat ant.** Your turn. Say that sentence. Get ready. (Signal.) *It is a fat ant.*

b. Now you're going to say it the slow way. Get ready. (Signal for each word as the children say:) *It* (pause) *is* (pause) *a* (pause) *fat* (pause) *ant.*

• (Repeat until firm.)

c. Everybody, write the sentence. Spell each word the right way. ✔

SPELLING LESSON 109

WORD WRITING
EXERCISE 1

Children write **see**

You're going to write the word **see.** Think about the sounds in (pause) **see** and write the word. ✔

> **To Correct** _____
> 1. Say the sounds in **see.** (Signal.) *sss ēēē.*
> 2. Say the sounds the hard way. (Signal.) *sss* (pause) *ēēē* (pause) *ēēē.*
> 3. Write the word **see.** ✔

EXERCISE 2

Children write **barn, bill, pill**

a. You're going to write the word (pause) **barn.** Say the sounds you write for (pause) **barn.** Get ready. (Signal for each sound as the children say:) *b* (pause) *aaa* (pause) *rrr* (pause) *nnn.* (The children are to pause two seconds between the sounds.)
- (Repeat until firm.)

b. Everybody, write the word (pause) **barn.** ✔

c. Now you're going to write the word (pause) **bill.** Say the sounds you write for (pause) **bill.** Get ready. (Signal for each sound as the children say:) *b* (pause) *iii* (pause) *lll* (pause) *lll.* (The children are to pause two seconds between the sounds.)
- (Repeat until firm.)

d. Everybody, write the word (pause) **bill.** ✔

e. Next you're going to write the word (pause) **pill.** Say the sounds you write for (pause) **pill.** Get ready. (Signal for each sound as the children say:) *p* (pause) *iii* (pause) *lll* (pause) *lll.* (The children are to pause two seconds between the sounds.)

- (Repeat until firm.)

f. Everybody, write the word (pause) **pill.** ✔

EXERCISE 3

Children write **it**

You're going to write the word **it.** Think about the sounds in (pause) **it** and write the word. ✔

EXERCISE 4

Children write **pit**

a. You're going to write the word **pit.** Listen. **Pit.** Saying the sounds in (pause) **pit** the hard way. Get ready. (Signal for each sound as the children say:) *p* (pause) *iii* (pause) *t.* (The children are to pause two seconds between the sounds.)

- (Repeat until firm.)

b. Everybody, write the word (pause) **pit.** ✔

SENTENCE WRITING
EXERCISE 5

Children write a sentence

a. Listen to this sentence. **We will win a car.** Your turn. Say that sentence. Get ready. (Signal.) *We will win a car.*

b. Now you're going to say it the slow way. Get ready. (Signal for each word as the children say:) *We* (pause) *will* (pause) *win* (pause) *a* (pause) *car.*

- (Repeat until firm.)

c. Everybody, write the sentence. Spell each word the right way. ✔

SPELLING LESSON 110

WORD WRITING
EXERCISE 1

Children write **bar, pill, will**

a. You're going to write the word (pause) **bar.** Say the sounds you write for (pause) **bar.** Get ready. (Signal for each sound as the children say:) *b* (pause) *aaa* (pause) *rrr.* (The children are to pause two seconds between the sounds.)

- (Repeat until firm.)
  b. Everybody, write the word (pause) **bar.** ✔
  c. Now you're going to write the word (pause) **pill.** Say the sounds you write for (pause) **pill.** Get ready. (Signal for each sound as the children say:) *p* (pause) *iii* (pause) *lll* (pause) *lll.* (The children are to pause two seconds between the sounds.)
- (Repeat until firm.)
  d. Everybody, write the word (pause) **pill.** ✔
  e. Next you're going to write the word (pause) **will.** Say the sounds you write for (pause) **will.** Get ready. (Signal for each sound as the children say:) *www* (pause) *iii* (pause) *lll* (pause) *lll.* (The children are to pause two seconds between the sounds.)
- (Repeat until firm.)
  f. Everybody, write the word (pause) **will.** ✔

EXERCISE 2

Children write **ham, bit, land**

a. You're going to write the word **ham.** Think about the sounds in (pause) **ham** and write the word. ✔

To Correct

1. Say the sounds in **ham.** (Signal.) *haaammm.*
2. Say the sounds the hard way. (Signal.) *h* (pause) *aaa* (pause) *mmm.*
3. Write the word **ham.** ✔

b. (Repeat step *a* for **bit** and **land.**)

SENTENCE WRITING
EXERCISE 3

Children write a sentence

a. Listen to this sentence. **He had mud on him.** Your turn. Say that sentence. Get ready. (Signal.) *He had mud on him.*
b. Now you're going to say it the slow way. Get ready. (Signal for each word as the children say:) *He* (pause) *had* (pause) *mud* (pause) *on* (pause) *him.*
- (Repeat until firm.)
c. Everybody, write the sentence. Spell each word the right way. ✔

SPELLING LESSON 111

WORD WRITING
EXERCISE 1

Children write **but**

You're going to write the word **but.** Think about the sounds in (pause) **but** and write the word. ✔

To Correct

1. Say the sounds in **but.** (Signal.) *buuut.*
2. Say the sounds the hard way. (Signal.) *b* (pause) *uuu* (pause) *t.*
3. Write the word **but.** ✔

EXERCISE 2

Children write **bar**

a. You're going to write the word (pause) **bar.** Say the sounds you write for (pause) **bar.** Get ready. (Signal for each sound as the children say:) *b* (pause) *aaa* (pause) *rrr.* (The children are to pause two seconds between the sounds.)
- (Repeat until firm.)
b. Everybody, write the word (pause) **bar.** ✔

EXERCISE 3

Children write **his, see, barn, and**

a. You're going to write the word **his.** Think about the sounds in (pause) **his** and write the word. ✔

To Correct _____

> 1. Say the sounds the hard way. (Signal.) *h* (pause) *iii* (pause) *sss.*
> 2. Write the word **his.** ✔

b. You're going to write the word **see.** Think about the sounds in (pause) **see** and write the word. ✔

To Correct _____

> 1. Say the sounds in **see.** (Signal.) *Ssseee.*
> 2. Say the sounds the hard way. (Signal.) *Sss* (pause) *eee* (pause) *eee.*
> 3. Write the word **see.** ✔

c. (Repeat step b for **barn** and **and.**)

SENTENCE WRITING
EXERCISE 4

Children write a sentence

a. Listen to this sentence. **We are on the farm.** Your turn. Say that sentence. Get ready. (Signal.) *We are on the farm.*

b. Now you're going to say it the slow way. Get ready. (Signal for each word as the children say:) *We* (pause) *are* (pause) *on* (pause) *the* (pause) *farm.*

- (Repeat until firm.)

c. Everybody, write the sentence. Spell each word the right way. ✔